WILFRED OWEN

Wilfred Owen with Arthur Newboult, Edinburgh, 1917.

WILFRED OWEN

THE LAST YEAR

1917–1918

Dominic Hibberd

CONSTABLE · LONDON

First published in Great Britian 1992
by Constable and Company Limited
3 The Lanchesters, 162 Fulham Palace Road
London W6 9ER
Copyright © 1992 Dominic Hibberd
Paperback edition 1993
Reprinted 1994
The right of Dominic Hibberd to be
identified as the author of this work
has been asserted by him in accordance
with the Copyright, Designs and Patents Act 1988
ISBN 0 09 472900 X
Set in Monophoto Photina 11pt by
Servis Filmsetting Ltd, Manchester
Printed in Great Britain by
St Edmundsbury Press Ltd
Bury St Edmunds, Suffolk

A CIP catalogue record for this book
is available from the British Library

CONTENTS

INTRODUCTION

ON 1 October 1918, Wilfred Owen became one of the first Allied company commanders to break into the German Army's last prepared defences. Soaked in the blood of his servant, who had been wounded in the first hour of the attack, he got his men through the wire and captured a machine gun, turning it on the enemy. For two nights and a day, he crawled about in – and in front of – the shallow trenches of the Hindenburg Reserve system, organizing resistance to counter-attacks, sending back prisoners, and attending to the wounded. Early on the morning of the 3rd, he led his exhausted company back to safety, finding his direction by the stars. He was a very different soldier from the nerve-ridden casualty who had been sent home, shell-shocked and suspected of cowardice, in June 1917. As a poet, too, he was different: in that June he had been working on a sentimental ballad about knights in armour, but just before he went into the Hindenburg Line he finished the last and best of his war poems, 'Spring Offensive'.

The change Owen had gone through in the last year of his life was due to two people above all, Arthur Brock and Siegfried Sassoon. Brock, his shell-shock doctor, had taught him how to reintegrate himself through work and will power, and Sassoon had given him his subject, 'War, and the pity of War'. Both Brock and Sassoon believed that poetry should serve social ends, whereas Owen had tended to think of it as an end in itself. In June 1917 he had written a sonnet, 'The Fates', which said that the pursuit of 'Beauty' was the best escape from life's realities, but nearly a year later he declared a contrary view: 'Above all, I am not concerned with Poetry'.

Owen's reformed attitude as a poet was closely related to his understanding of what it meant to be a soldier. 'The Fates' was composed for his cousin, who was a civilian and who came to represent not only the old kind of poetry which had to be left behind but also the civilian lack of understanding which had to be attacked. Writing to his cousin soon after the fighting in the Hindenburg Line, Owen reproached him for not being 'in the flesh with Us nor in the spirit against war'; by

'Us' he meant both true poets like himself and Sassoon, and honourable soldiers like the men around him.

In October 1918 he knew that there were over thirty poems in his desk at Shrewsbury, all written during the previous year, which would speak to future generations. During that year he had been recognized by some of the most promising writers of his own generation and been welcomed into a distinguished literary circle in London. His new friends gave him confidence, sharing his ideas and feelings, so that he was freed from the stifling respectability of his provincial upbringing and enabled to find himself as man and poet. Yet none of these changes involved denying his past. He learned to make use of his early writing, and he maintained his links with home; and the trench experiences which had nearly destroyed him were transformed through courage and hard work into material for poetry.

Wilfred Edward Salter Owen was born on 18 March 1893, the eldest of four children. His parents, Tom and Susan, were living in comfort with Susan's father at Oswestry; Tom was a badly-paid railway clerk, but his father-in-law had been prosperous. In later years Owen could just remember the Oswestry house, with its spacious rooms and grounds. His grandfather died in 1897, leaving much less money than had been expected, and the family moved to a dismal area of Birkenhead, where Tom became a stationmaster. From then on there was an unending struggle to keep a footing in the middle class. Owen's letters and the copious memoirs of his brother, Harold, often reveal the anxieties about money and social status which the children absorbed from their parents. Owen longed to go to a public school and Oxford, and it meant a great deal to him in 1917–18 to be accepted by people from that world. His own education never went further than the Birkenhead Institute and then, when his father moved to a better job, the Technical School at Shrewsbury.

By the time he left school he was writing verse, dreaming of becoming a poet, and going through a period of special devotion to Keats. His debt to Keats has often been exaggerated; he thought Shelley a greater genius and was influenced by many other nineteenth-century writers. His avowal at the end of 1917 that he had always felt 'sympathy for the oppressed' was in origin a literary attitude, learned from Shelley, Wordsworth, Dickens, and Ruskin. Ruskin also taught him that a poet

Left: Tom and Susan Owen, photographed in Oswestry.

Right: Wilfred, their first child.

Susan Owen with Mary, and a nursemaid with Harold, Wilfred standing between them, c.1897.

Wilfred in uniform.

Tom and Susan with their four children: Wilfred, aged 12; Mary, aged 10; Harold, aged 7; and Colin, aged 5. Scarborough, summer 1905.

Left: Wilfred in his teens; *right*: as lay assistant, Dunsden Vicarage, 1912.

should know about the world as a whole, plants and stones as well as people, so Owen was keen on botany, geology, and astronomy. Underlying all his thinking in his early years was the simple evangelical faith he shared with his mother. He read the Bible daily and was a regular church-goer, developing a sense of mission which outlasted his youthful piety and eventually found expression in his fervent preaching against war.

University fees being out of the question, he had to try for a scholarship. After a brief period as a pupil-teacher in 1911, he became an unpaid assistant to the Vicar of Dunsden, near Reading, in return for promised tuition. He had already begun to lose his religious convictions, and the contrast between village poverty and 'the Silence, the State, and the Stiffness' of life in the vicarage made matters worse. Poetry became increasingly valuable, his own as a means of releasing feelings, and other people's as a source of guidance. His first cousin, Leslie Gunston, who lived nearby, became his literary confidant and was to remain his closest friend until 1917. They took to writing poems in competition with each other, choosing for their first subject the swifts flying round

Listening to Laurent Tailhade
lecture, Bagnères-de-Bigorre,
August 1914.

the vicarage, symbols of freedom and energy.

A village Revival at the end of 1912 forced the lay assistant to take a
first step towards his own freedom; amid the flurry of conversions and
prayer meetings, and after much inner torment, he told the Vicar that
Christianity was inconsistent with science and poetry. He took leave of
the parish children, his best friends at Dunsden – one of the boys was to
haunt his poetry for years afterwards as an image of love, youth, and
loss, – and went home in a state of collapse, suffering from what seem to
have been severe nightmares, precursors of his war dreams. His mother
nursed him back to health. In the summer he took a scholarship and
failed it.

In September 1913 he went to Bordeaux as an English teacher,
putting himself up the social scale by hinting that he was waiting to go
up to Oxford and that his father was a baronet. By the time war broke

In his new uniform as Second Lieutenant, June 1916, photographed by his
uncle, John Gunston.

out in August 1914, he was living with a family in the Pyrenees. Fit and brown after helping with the hay harvest in that marvellously fine summer, he met and enchanted a famous poet, Laurent Tailhade, an old Decadent and anarchist, sometime friend of Verlaine and ornament of the Paris *salons*. Owen's reactions to the war were those of an Aesthete and lover of France, and he made no attempt to return home. He began to read French literature and to experiment with verse in Tailhade's style. When he first returned to England in May 1915, it was only briefly, as a sales representative for a scent manufacturer.

Recruiting propaganda in London stirred his conscience, so that he began to think of enlisting. The few poems he wrote about the war before 1917 show little sign of his later convictions; one contains a description of Germany as a 'vast Beast' and another says it is 'sweet' and 'meet' to 'die in war with brothers'. Quoting the posters, he told Gunston he felt obliged to follow 'The Only Way'. With his background, he would have had difficulty in getting a commission, except that the Army regarded time spent abroad as some compensation for the lack of a gentlemanly education. He gave up his tutoring in the autumn and considered becoming a munitions worker, but finally decided to enlist as a cadet in the Artists' Rifles.

His training began in Bloomsbury, where he got to know another well-known poet, Harold Monro, proprietor of the Poetry Bookshop; Monro read his poems and gave good advice about them. By June 1916 Owen was judged fit to become an officer in the Territorials (hence the 'T' visible on his uniform in some photographs). He was commissioned as a second lieutenant in the 5th Battalion, Manchester Regiment, and spent the rest of the year training in England. On 30 December he was sent out to the base camp at Etaples.

Men in transit at Etaples were put through a deliberately harsh burst of training, but nothing could prepare newcomers for the actuality of trench warfare. Owen was posted to the 2nd Manchesters, a Regular battalion, and went into the line near Beaumont Hamel. Marked for capture on the first day of the Somme offensive in July, the village had finally been taken in November after appalling slaughter. Bones were frozen into the shattered roads. Almost his first task was to occupy a flooded German dug-out in No Man's Land. The two entrances faced the enemy lines and one had already been blown in. For over two days he and his men huddled in the rising water, expecting to be buried or drowned. They almost were buried when a shell just missed the

15   ÉTRETAT. — Les Falaises — LL.

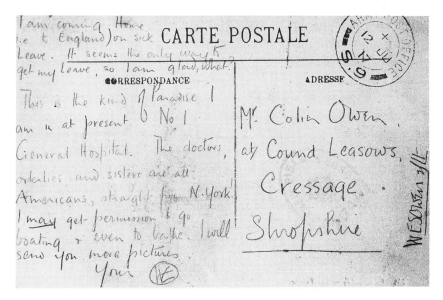

Postcard from Owen to his brother, Colin, from hospital in Etretat, 12 June 1917.

remaining shaft, blinding the sentry. It did not occur to Owen at this stage that experiences like this might be fit subjects for poetry, but his letters were vivid and angry. He shared most soldiers' resentment at ignorant civilians and 'shirkers', the fit men at home who had evaded military service. At the end of January, his seniors may have thought he needed a rest; he was sent on a course well behind the lines.

Returning to the front in March, he fell into some kind of hole and apparently lay there concussed for several days. After a fortnight in a casualty clearing station at Cerisy[1] on the Somme Canal, he rejoined the battalion on the hills above St Quentin. The Germans were making a planned retreat to their new 'Hindenburg Line' and the city was impregnable behind massive fortifications, even though Owen was close enough to see the cathedral. The battalion fought well, capturing trenches, guns, and a well-defended quarry, but their successes meant little. He led his platoon through an artillery barrage, only to find that the enemy had withdrawn a stage further. Shaken after days under fire, he fell asleep on a railway embankment, somewhere near Savy Wood, and was blown into the air by a shell, a near-miss that seems to have left him sheltering helplessly, close to the dismembered remains of another officer.

When he got back to base, people noticed that he was trembling, confused, and stammering. It seems probable that his courage was called into question in some way by the CO, who may even have bluntly called him a coward.[2] The doctor diagnosed shell-shock or 'neurasthenia', and Owen was sent back to Cerisy, and then to a hospital at Etretat, where it was decided that the right place for him would be Craiglockhart War Hospital, near Edinburgh. Had the decision gone another way, some of the finest war poems in the English language might never have been written.

— 1 —

RETURN TO ENGLAND

HAVING spent the first four months of 1917 on active service, Owen spent the next six as a hospital patient. For a man of his light physique and sensitive temperament, he had not done badly, but his time in the front line had amounted to only a few weeks; the Regulars of the 2nd Battalion would have expected an officer to keep going for longer than that. Shell-shock was still not fully understood or recognized. Many people, especially senior Army men, regarded it as a form of malingering. Wounds in the mind were much less glorious than wounds in the flesh, and the least hint of cowardice was a disgrace.

Owen asked his mother not to let it be generally known that he was a casualty, and after the war his family and friends did their best to cover up the details. It is difficult now to guess what state he was in when he arrived in England. Some of the people he met in the summer recorded a few memories: Siegfried Sassoon said he had a stammer; Robert Graves said he was in 'a very shaky condition'; Arthur Newboult thought he had seemed 'nervy and highly strung'; and Mary Gray said he was liable to acute depression and self-distrust. Both Graves and Mrs Gray added that the 'accusation' of cowardice preyed on his mind, although Mrs Gray described it as a 'painful delusion'.

Owen himself said that nightmares were his worst symptom. His dreams were of dark caves, dug-outs, and distorted landscapes, haunted by the tortured, accusing faces of the men he had been responsible for – a soldier choking to death in sudden gas, the horribly blinded sentry at Beaumont Hamel, his leaderless platoon at Savy Wood. Shell-shock symptoms tended to emerge wherever a man was most vulnerable: Owen had always been prone to bad dreams, visions of hell and deathly faces.

Being back in England took some getting used to. He was based for about a week in a huge military hospital near Southampton and spent the days roaming about, 'absorbing Hampshire'. Leslie Gunston came down one afternoon from a camp at Hazeley Down, near Winchester, where he was doing his bit for the war by helping with the catering in a YMCA hut. Owen could not feel at ease in the old way, pleased though

Leslie Gunston.

he was to see his cousin. Gunston had been excused military service on the grounds of a 'mitral murmur', a suspected irregularity in the heart valves, and his elder brother, Gordon, had also remained a civilian.[1] Owen disapproved. He had probably been thinking of the Gunstons in April when he had said that the battalion felt 'bitterly towards those in England who might relieve us, but will not'. Doctors had been worried about his own heart before the war, but he had joined up. There was a galling contrast between his own guilt at having failed and his cousin's apparently easy conscience at having never even put himself to the test.

For the moment Owen put such thoughts aside. One of his diversions during the previous few months had been to compose sonnets on

Two paintings in the Royal Academy Summer Exhibition, 1917: Charles Butler, *Blood and Iron*, and Charles Sims, *Greater love hath no man*.

subjects chosen by himself, Gunston, and a friend of theirs: 'Happiness', 'Golden Hair', 'Sunrise'. Both cousins had been inclined to think of poetry as something separate from ordinary words and experience; they were still writing as late Victorians, using Swinburnian diction and enjoying art for art's sake. Owen had recently begun a pseudo-medieval ballad, the sort of project his cousin would be sure to like. It seemed an appropriate task for someone about to go to Scotland and he busied himself with it, scribbling pages about the Lady Yolande, rival knights, and a beautiful page boy. Serious writing could not yet be contemplated.

He hoped for three weeks' leave, to include a visit to Shrewsbury, but the doctors allowed no time for it. He was instructed to travel direct to Edinburgh on 25 June, and all he could squeeze out of that was an afternoon in London. He visited the Royal Academy Summer Exhibition, as he always did when he had the chance. Two conspicuous pictures that year were Charles Butler's *Blood and Iron*, showing the Kaiser riding into battle and glancing down contemptuously at Christ ministering to dying Belgians, and Charles Sims's *Greater love hath no man*, a crucifixion scene in which the traditional figures were replaced by a wounded soldier and his mourning family. Images like these of the German 'Beast' and the British soldier-Christ were very common at the time, and Owen had used both. He was unimpressed by the exhibition, perhaps because he noticed an absurdly fanciful painting by Caton Woodville, showing the Manchesters capturing guns near St Quentin.

He went on to the Shamrock Tea Rooms,

> perhaps the most eminently respectable exclusive and secluded in Town. There was the usual deaf old lady and her Companion holding forth upon the new curate. I happen to know that a few stories higher in the same building is an Opium Den. I have not investigated. But I know. That's London.

He had always been fond of secrets. After tea he walked up Bond Street to Pope and Bradley, the military tailors, to order some new trousers, his uniform having suffered in the realities of the action at St Quentin. On the way he met a conceited colonel from the 2nd Manchesters whom he particularly disliked, and knew very well that the man's affability concealed contempt for a junior with a provincial accent and a record of doubtful courage. 'To meet him in my first hour in town. Alas! This, also, is London!'

The colonel's chilly eye and the tailor's tape measure sized up a not very soldierly figure. Owen was fit after eighteen months in the Army, his face tanned a deep reddish-brown and his bearing correctly military, but he was a small man, under five foot six, and at twenty-four still very young-looking, despite his little moustache and the premature streaks of grey in his close-cropped hair. His manner was shy and self-effacing, qualities no doubt accentuated by shell-shock. Subalterns were urged to be 'bloodthirsty' and were even asked the memorable question, 'How offensive are you?', but Owen had no aggressiveness. One of his fellow lieutenants, John Foulkes, was struck by his 'curious lack of growl' in 1918, and another, H.R. Bate, who was with him in camp in 1915 and 1918, remembered him as silent, withdrawn, and sometimes bullied by his seniors.

Owen's letters home naturally give no hint that he was ever bullied. As it was his family who controlled public perception of him after his death, he has sometimes been written about in flattering, even heroic terms, to the irritation of Bate and perhaps others. It is clear even from

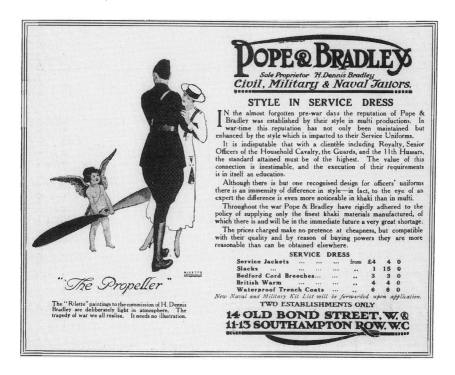

A characteristic advertisement for Pope & Bradley (*The Bystander*, 20 June 1917).

his letters that he tended to avoid the sort of social activities and conversation that most officers gave their time to. He had an excellent sense of humour, yet Bate never saw him smile. Only a very few people were allowed to know his inner self and his passion for poetry. Foulkes once happened to quote some Keats to him and noticed how his face 'shone with wonder and delight'. Friends remembered how well he read verse aloud (Sassoon described his voice as 'velvety'), and several memoirs comment on his eyes, 'dark in their colour', Osbert Sitwell said, 'and deep in their meaning'. In June 1917 he still had few literary friends in England; he had published nothing and written little worth publishing. As both poet and soldier, he was entirely undistinguished. It was as well to appear as ordinary as possible to arrogant colonels, even when exchanging pleasantries in Bond Street.

— 2 —

HOSPITAL

'A decayed Hydro'

OWEN caught the overnight train from King's Cross, and reached Edinburgh on 26 June. He had seen the city before; after a huge breakfast at the North British Hotel above the station, he went out into Princes Street and admired the view of the castle, which 'looked more than ever a Hallucination, with the morning sun behind it'. He was not free to prolong such pleasures, though, and soon he was in a taxi for the two-and-a-half miles to Craiglockhart. Having registered and found his room, he wrote home as a first duty, reporting cheerlessly that he was in 'a decayed Hydro, far too full of officers, some of whom I know'. It was not pleasant to be recognized in this place of failures. He went out to 'take the lie of the land'.[1]

Craiglockhart War Hospital for Neurasthenic Officers had only been in existence for about nine months. The Army had taken over a hydropathic sanatorium, constructed in 1877–80 when 'water cures' had been in fashion. The building occupied a magnificent site, the main façade and belvedere tower looking north-west over a great sweep of moors to the Firth of Forth and distant mountains. The original facilities had included Turkish and swimming baths, and 'ladies' and gentlemen's special Bath-rooms, with all the varieties of hot and cold plunge, vapour, spray, needle, douche, and electrical baths, with special galvanic apparatus'. There was a recreation room with a small proscenium stage and several vast lounges. The twelve acres of ornamental grounds included a bowling green and a half-mile cycle track. Despite these amenities, the place had never prospered, perhaps because it was too much exposed to wind and rain, or too close to the suburbs.

Owen explored the long corridors without enthusiasm. There was a pervasive reek of stale tobacco smoke. Officers were playing bridge or reading newspapers in the shabby common rooms. At least there were

The North British Station Hotel and the east end of Princes Street, Edinburgh.

Princes Street, looking west from the North British Hotel.

Craiglockhart Hydropathic: guests on the bowling green before 1917.

Craiglockhart from the air, probably in the 1920s.

books: the hydro's stock of old novels and encyclopaedias had survived, and there was a silence room where someone attended daily to lend books from a circulating library in the city. Noticeboards in the hall announced numerous activities run by the Officers' Club, from poultry-

The drawings in this chapter are from the Craiglockhart magazine, *The Hydra*. They were made by Lieutenant A. Berrington for the New Series in October 1917 to illustrate reports on Notes and News (the hospital notice boards), the Field Club (p.26), Concerts (p.30), the Debating Society (Owen was apparently on the committee, p.35), Golf (p.38), and Departures (the three officers are bound for Permanent Base, Light Duties, and General Service, p.56).

keeping to language classes. Where people had once come for rest-cures, everyone was now urged to keep busy. Yet too many of the patients seemed to be drifting about aimlessly. They stuttered when spoken to. Some were unsteady on their legs. It was unwise to slam doors or talk about the front. Some cases were in a bad way, with vacant eyes and hands constantly on the move.

> – These are men whose minds the Dead have ravished.
> Memory fingers in their hair of murders,
> Multitudinous murders they once witnessed.

So Owen was to remember them in 1918.

The hospital grounds seemed largely given over to sport, except for the hen-house and some allotments, where patients and local people were raising flowers and vegetables. The ruined 'castle', presented as a romantic feature in the old hydro brochure, looked no more than a tumbledown cart-shed. Behind it, though, the hill rose abruptly to an open stretch of moorland. Owen would have been reminded of his beloved Shropshire; if he scrambled up through the long grass, he would have found Midlothian spread out below, east to the skyline of the old city, and south over the golf courses to Swanston and the green wall of the Pentland Hills.

When he went to bed that first night, he put his revolver beside him out of habit. In the morning it had gone.[2] The nurses could not allow inmates to have weapons. By night the hospital became a place of terror. Dreading the memories that dreams would revive, men kept themselves awake, smoking incessantly, despite admonitions from the staff. When sleep finally overcame them, they were at the front again, struggling in vain to escape the experiences that had broken through their self-control. Sudden shouts and hurrying feet would echo down the corridors. Only a few days after Owen arrived, he wrote to his cousin that he had sat up reading until three in the morning. Later he described himself as one of 'the weary who don't want rest' and was glad when the nurses gave up trying to cajole him into turning his light off.

'I am not able to settle down here without seeing Mother', he told Nellie Bulman, an old friend of Mrs Owen's, on 1 July. 'I feel a sort of reserve and suspense about everything I do.' Mrs Bulman had been his hostess on his only previous visit to Scotland. She sent him strawberries and cream, and her daughter, Blanche, arranged to meet him in town. In his second week at Craiglockhart, Mrs Owen came up from Shrewsbury. It was agreed that she should stay for about a week with the Newboult family, friends of hers and Mrs Bulman, at Summerside Place, Leith, and then go on to Mrs Bulman at Yetholm for a short holiday, before returning to Leith for a few days more. She thought of seeing another acquaintance, but her son objected, impatient as always when she wanted to spend time with her friends rather than with him:

> Personally I don't see what Auntie Bobs has got to do with my seeing my Mother on my return from war. If I had foreseen Auntie Bobs when I was sinking in the mud or coming-to after the Embankment-Shell-Shock it would have been the last straw.

Mother and son arranged to meet at the Caledonian Hotel at the west end of Princes Street. When he saw her 'gliding' up to him, his 'exultation' reminded him of his feelings after getting through the barrage. He had not seen her for over six months. She took her veil off and he noticed how grey she was: 'the ashes of all your Sacrifices: for Father, for me, and for all of us'.

His relationship with her had always been passionately close, too much so as he had sometimes admitted, but since January he had

A Scottish holiday, 1912. *Below*:
Mrs Nellie Bulman (left) invited the
Owens to stay with her family at
Kelso. Her daughter, Blanche (third
from left), took Wilfred to see
Flodden Field; John, the eldest son
(the photographer), showed him
round Edinburgh. Bill, the second
son (seated right), and Walter
Forrest (Blanche's fiancé, standing)
were killed in the war a few years
later. Harold, Susan, and Mary
Owen sit together in the
photograph, with Colin on the
ground and Tom standing behind.
Right: Wilfred arrived after the rest
of his family, so John took another
photograph, less successfully.

grown away from her, strong though their love still was. As he had written in workings for his first poem after Beaumont Hamel, the old happiness of being a 'Mother's boy' was unreturning. He had seen and done things beyond her understanding. Nevertheless, the moment when he saw her in the Caledonian was the beginning of his cure. They renewed their old companionship; he took her on 'conducted tours' of the city, and she came up to the hospital to attend a concert. He endured afternoons at the Newboults as politely as he could, resenting having to share her company but pleased when the seven-year-old Arthur adopted him as a friend. By the time she left, his 'reserve and suspense' had gone; helped by his doctor, he began to fill his time with purposeful activity.

Dr Brock

When he reported to Dr Brock's room on his first morning at Craiglockhart, the new patient found himself being studied – and lectured to – by a lean, earnest man with deep-set eyes and a nose like an axe-blade.[3] Arthur Brock's RAMC uniform sat awkwardly on his bony frame and had never been near a battlefield; his authority came from his seriousness and learning, not from his rank. As he talked, he drew examples from Greek medicine, Italian art, or modern social theory, as though there were no boundaries between subjects. He seemed more like a tutor than a doctor.

Before long Brock was referring to the picture above his table; like the vision-testing card on the bookshelf below, it was there as a professional aid. He thought art should be useful, not an end in itself. (Perhaps it was at this point that Owen began to wonder whether a true poet should be 'concerned with Poetry'.) The print showed two wrestlers, one lifting the other off the ground. The man in the air, legs flailing, was Antaeus, son of the Earth; he had seemed invincible until his opponent, Hercules, discovered that his strength would fail as soon as his contact with his mother, the Earth, was broken. Here was an image of shell-shock: the soldier had lost touch with real life and would be destroyed by the war giant unless he could get his feet back on the ground. The comparison was apt for Owen, who had been hurled off the ground by shell-blast at

Captain A.J. Brock, RAMC.

Savy Wood. Brock said that what was true for people was true throughout nature, that the organism must maintain vital contact with its environment. Patients had to heal themselves by their own efforts; he could only give advice. Treatment would be by work-cure or, in his pre-war coinage, 'ergotherapy'.

The doctor made careful observations, noting Owen's interest in literature and the earth sciences, and he seems to have taken the chance to meet Mrs Owen. He would have discovered the powerful bond between mother and son, and the remoteness of the father, but he was no Freudian; if he spent any time discussing sexuality, it would have been because Owen was repressing guilt about that as well as about events in France. Those events had to be uncovered quickly: the longer they lay buried, the greater the risk of permanent mental damage. Brock may have used the technique known as 'abreaction', which helped patients to release inner terrors by reliving them (men would sometimes hurl themselves shrieking to the floor, hearing the shells bursting round them again). More probably, he had no need to go beyond his preferred method of reasoned conversation. He was positive, not to say relentless. Owen had to reconnect himself with his past and put it to work.

Even war dreams could be useful. There is a scribbled note in Brock's copy of Edgar Allan Poe's poems which reads: '*Nightmares* – Note that Strindberg (supported in this by his countryman Swedenborg), unlike *Gérard de Nerval, E.A. Poe, & Baudelaire*, came to realise the *utility* of a period of nightmare for purgation of the soul, & was not, like them, overcome by it.' Bad dreams were an expression of failure and guilt. The way to deal with them was to face up strenuously to what they represented and resolve to do better. Owen's letters from Craiglockhart record that his 'Barrage'd Nights' steadily decreased; at the same time, his poetic ability began to develop with extraordinary speed, probably with the doctor's encouragement.

Brock had no difficulty in deciding on the first exercise for a young poet who found the theory of ergotherapy interesting. Owen was sent away to write an essay on the Outlook Tower. He took the tram into town and found the tower at the top of the Royal Mile, near the castle. It was an odd, fascinating place, a tall medieval house adapted as a centre for sociological studies. Here Brock's ideas could be seen as part of a complete world-view. Behind it all lay the charismatic personality of the tower's owner and organizer, Patrick Geddes, a celebrated sociologist and scientist, Brock's friend and mentor for many years. The threepenny guide book explained the tower in Geddes's unmistakable style. He wanted people to look at their environment afresh, renewing vital contact with it: 'to fully and truly understand our region, we must seek the help of all the specialists, from astronomer to historian, from physician to poet' – and we must recognize that all specialisms are part of one great whole. In the next few months, thanks to Brock the physician, Owen was to meet the Astronomer Royal and a local historian, Lord Guthrie.

The tour of the building was designed to be a spiritual journey, which started on the roof. Visitors were directed to study the view of Edinburgh and its environs, and then to enter a darkened room, the Camera Obscura, to look down into a large dish, where panoramic images of the city were projected from a device in the cupola.[4] The tour continued downwards through the tower, passing a 'Cell', furnished with a single chair, where the serious visitor was invited to pause for meditation. Owen evidently made use of this, for a passage about the soul in his battered copy of *Gems from Hilaire Belloc* is marked 'Outlook Tower   The Cell'. Then came a sequence of exhibitions, with elaborate globes, diagrams, and pictures, so that by the time

A FIRST VISIT
TO THE
OUTLOOK TOWER.

Price Threepence

visitors reached the street they had been made to think about themselves in relation to the city, the world, and the universe.

Owen read his essay to Brock on 14 July. Some of his rough notes survive, including his introduction:

I perceived that this Tower was a symbol: an Allegory, not a historic structure but a poetic form. I had supposed it to be a museum, and found it [a] philosophical poem: when I had stood within its walls an hour I became aware of a soul, and the continuity of its idea from room to room, and from storey to storey was an epic.

Its very position and its build are symbolic. 'There are primal things which move us,' say[s] H Belloc. A Tower far off arrests a man's eye always; it is more than a break in the sky-line; it is an enemy's watch, or the rallying point of a defence to whose aid we are summoned. However this also is symbolic: that the Tower, though dominant over the whole champaign, is not isolated. The roofs of all the city lean against it, and on its skirts hang the hands of the children of the very poor. It is indeed a watch and a stronghold. But its power is in the opening of its doors: and so it takes its enemies. For it[s] chief enemy is the Spirit of exclusiveness. It stands to disarm The Exclusive, by which in Science, I mean the over-specialist locking himself in a groove, in Letters the pedant in Religion the Fanatic in Ethics the Egotist and in Society the Snob. They are all its enemies, more even than Ignorance, Indifference, and Ugliness.

The Tower is suggestive of the great Method [of] Philosophical Thinking which is Correlation or Coordination.

Brock may have had reservations about the Belloc-like style of the essay, but he would have been pleased that a poet and soldier had responded to the Tower in a poetic and soldierly way, seeing it as a symbol and fortress. Owen had made another step towards wholeness.

The next task was to write a poem on Antaeus. The encyclopaedias in the library were not informative, so Owen decided to restrict himself to a sonnet. Then the image of the two wrestlers fired him, and he turned out a long blank-verse narrative, full of the energy the doctor wanted to generate.

> As pythons shudder, bridling-in their spite
> So trembled that Antaeas with held strength,
> While Heracles, – the thews and cordage of his thighs
> Straitened and strained beyond the utmost stretch
> From quivering heel to haunch like sweating hawsers –
> But only staggered backward.

It may well be that Owen continued to show Brock new writing as part of ergotherapy, discussing both content and technique. He seems to have developed a new system of rhyming during his first month or so at Craiglockhart. He also drafted some curious poems about his innermost fantasies, visions of blood-sacrifice and dying youth; these show him already facing up to what the doctor called '"the phantoms of the mind"'.[5]

Part of a letter from Owen to Gunston, late July 1917.

The work-cure

Brock wanted to set up a core programme of ergotherapy for all his patients. With Owen as a founder-member, he started the Field Club on 13 July and later, probably in August, the Boys' Training Club, two organizations which provided respectively for 'synoptic seeing' (seeing the world as a whole) and 'synergic action' (communal work), the two basic elements in the work-cure. Owen went on several Field Club expeditions, looking at stones and plants on the Pentlands. On 30 July he gave a Geddesian lecture on the question, 'Do Plants Think?', arguing that they do, because plants, like people, need to respond to their environment. He amused his audience with some topical

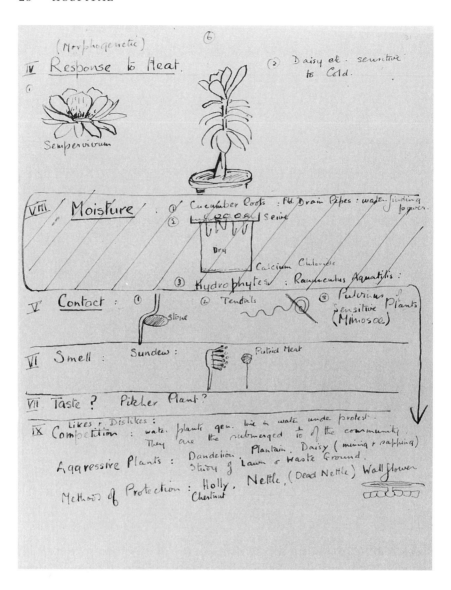

Some of Owen's notes for 'Do Plants Think?', 30 July 1917.

references – daisies mine and sap, the cabbage does no work (unlike Brock's patients), some plants show 'exaggerated reflexes' – and ended by quoting Tennyson and Mrs Browning, to demonstrate that the poets had seen the truth before the scientists. There was warm applause, and for a moment he felt the learned man he had always wanted to be.

We have seen enough (In conclusion) ~~I have tried~~ to show that the ascription [of a super-material Something: call it [spirit, mind : is not an poetic fancy, but that it is the last word of the ~~most~~ keenest of the Sciences : Biology. And the definite answer to the question : "What is it that thinks in ~~plants~~, growing tissue or if you like, for ~~plants~~? " if answered only with respect to a bean-plant, would solve the whole problem of life on this planet. As an old rustic said to me once: "The Roots of bein' are Bean Roots". The poets have seen it all along. They have even gone out of their province to insist upon it : for I do not consider ~~this~~ of Tennysons as Poetry : "Flower of the crannied wall, ... man is". (Mrs Browning) . . . . . Presented scientifically, it is ~~That sounds very pretty~~. startling. But to my mind the scientist has no right to be startled. If he is, then he is one of those pedants, who still linger in certain academic chairs of whom the greatest man Oxford ever turned out (turned out in the forcible sense, I mean) remarked: "I understand they need 6 months holiday in the year. Had I my way, they should take 12, and an extra day on leap-years." ~~Adaptation~~ The Theory of Evolution. Adaptation to Environment & the Survival of the Fittest may

Members of the Boys' Training Club were asked to work with scout groups (Baden Powell sent his approval) or to teach, mostly in the nearest board school, Tynecastle. All chose such subjects as map-reading, signalling, first aid, or physical drill, except Owen, who bravely pioneered a class in literature at the school. This combination of children and books was an excellent form of ergotherapy for him. He enjoyed it hugely, and his thirty-nine boys and their young teacher, Mrs

Swanston and the Pentland Hills.

Fullerton, seem to have adored him. He read *Hiawatha* with them and they built a wigwam; then he introduced them to R.L. Stevenson's *St Ives*.

Parts of *St Ives* are set in the Craiglockhart area and at Swanston Cottage, where Stevenson had spent childhood summers, so Owen and Mrs Fullerton took four of the boys to see the house. They had a picnic in the lee of a haystack, enjoying the view of Swanston and the hills, and walked back under the stars. He remembered this occasion as one of his happiest moments in Scotland. Next day, he revisited the house (it was hardly a cottage, having been built by eighteenth-century lawyers as a place for 'junketings') as the guest of the current tenant, Lord Guthrie, who had been a friend of Stevenson's.

Other ergotherapeutic activities included editing the hospital magazine, taking a course of German lessons, and visiting the observatory.
The editorship of *The Hydra* brought with it a seat on the Officers' Club
committee, so Owen found himself at the centre of affairs and he
became, as he said, 'one of the ones in the hospital'. Brock liked to
organize patients in pairs, each 'constituting himself a doctor' to the
other; Owen seems to have worked with a young subaltern called
Mayes, who had been at Craiglockhart since March[6]. Mayes helped
with the magazine, but his own enthusiasm was for acting; Owen took
minor parts in at least two plays.

Brock was keen that patients should feel themselves 'honorary
citizens' of Edinburgh. Although people tended to stare at the 'mad'
patients from Craiglockhart, who were conspicuous in blue armbands
and white tabs, many willing helpers had been found in the city. Mayes
introduced Owen to the Grays and the Steinthals, two families who
shared a large house in the New Town, and Owen came near to being
'mildly "lionised by Edinburgh Society"'. Behind the Georgian magnifi-
cence of St Bernard's Crescent, there was a modernity he had not seen
before. The drawing-room astonished him: 'black carpetless floor, white

St Bernard's Crescent, Edinburgh.

One of the 'Open Spaces' run by the Outlook Tower in the Edinburgh slums.

Henry Lintott, *Avatar*, 1917.

walls, solitary superb picture, grand piano, Empire sofa'. He met two artists who lived in the Crescent, Henry Lintott, painter of the solitary picture, and John Duncan. Lintott's *Avatar*, a romantic vision of a dead soldier being carried heavenwards by angels, had already drawn Owen's admiration at the Royal Scottish Academy. The Grays held 'perfect little' dinners for their new friend, at one of which he met the university librarian and accepted his offer of more German lessons. Surrounded by fine architecture, works of art, and talk of books and ideas, Owen was made to feel at home.

Ergotherapy required that the patient should make contact with the roughest levels of Edinburgh life, as well as with the most civilized. On Brock's instructions, Owen was shown round the 'Slum Gardens', oases of green established in the poorest quarters of the old city by the Outlook Tower's Open Spaces Committee.[7] His guide was a Miss Wyer, a keen Geddes disciple; she invited him to tea afterwards at her 'palatial' house

THE HYDRA.

EDITORIAL.

MANY of us who came to the Hydro slightly ill are now getting dangerously well.

Already we begin to see ourselves crouching before T.N.T., N.G., and other High and mighty Explosives, of which the one known as C.O. is not the least formidable.

In this excellent Concentration Camp we are fast recovering from the shock of coming to England. For some of us were not a little wounded by the apparent indifference of the public and the press, not indeed to our precious selves, but to the unimagined durances of the fit fellow in the line.

We were a little *too* piqued by the piquancy of smart women, and as for the dainty newspaper jokes concerning the men in the mud, we could not see them at all.

* * *

Perhaps it was that our eyes had been pained by the minute type of the roll of honour, and injured by the enormous headlines of Dreadful Dramatic Dream of Malcolm Murder.

* * *

Our reflections, like our reflexes, may have been exaggerated when, on first looking round England, we soliloquised thus :—

Who cares the Kaiser frowns imperially?
The exempted shriek at Charlie Chaplin's smirk.
The *Mirror* shows how Tommy smiles at work.
And if girls sigh, they sigh ethereally.
And wish the Push would get on less funereally.
Old Bill enlarges on his little jokes.
Punch is still grinning at the Derby blokes.
And Belloc prophecies of last year, serially.

* * *

If there is any one able to cure us of this cynicism it is our V.A.D.'s. They sigh often enough over us. We think it is time to thank them for their work in this Hospital. We do thank them, together with all those friends who send gifts, and who come to entertain us on Saturday evenings.

* * *

The Monday night meetings of the Field Club are not as well attended as they should be : perhaps because there are so many other attractive institutions. Anyhow, one no longer hears the cry : What is the Club doing for us ?

One contributor seems so well in love with the life here that he writes inquiring : Shall I mutter and stutter, and wangle my ticket ?

Or try another flutter, and go back and stick it ?

We should like to print more of this, but must first consult our Home Service Pocket Book, paragraph on " Licences, poetic, officers for the abuse of."

One more word about contributions. (The remarks in our last number were rather vague, not to say smoky.) *We want more topical* **articles** *and verse*. And whereas the plea of would-be contributors, when asked for their work, is that it is not yet finished, most pieces submitted are much too lengthy. It reminds us of a remark of the greatest man Oxford ever turned out (forcibly, we mean), which, slightly parodied, is this : The great poets are above the pains of careful endings. Thus, Homer ends with lines that might as well be in the middle of a passage ; Hesiod, one knows not how ; and *The Hydra*. the new voice from Craiglockhart, does not end at all, but is still going on.

1st & Passenger : Wot's a 'ydra?
2nd do. : A snake on a stick, first invented by
Moses; now the badge of the R.A.M.C.
1st do : I thought I was a place where yer
took life in bawths, in a number
insultin' to such as you an' me, but
right enough for officers 'ome from the
trenches.
3rd do. : Yer both wrong. A 'ydra's a 'undred-
'eaded serpent, and the 'eads grew again
as fast as cut off; signifying these 'ere
officers at Craiglockhart; for as soon as one
gets too uppish, like, they cut 'im off the
strength, an' another comes up in 'is place.

* * *

Above: Part of Owen's editorial for the 4 August number of *The Hydra*.

Left: Owen's *Hydra* editorial for 1 September, including a version of stanzas from the first draft of 'The Dead-Beat'.

in Rothesay Place. She and her friends seemed 'strange beings', but he was delighted to find that they shared his own ' – almost secret – views of such things as sculpture, state-craft, ethics, etc. etc'. Mrs Gray also took him slum-visiting, but they made an outlandish pair among the gloomy tenements, he in uniform and she in modern clothes which even he considered 'weird'. Socializing at the other end of the scale was more rewarding. He was grateful to the Army for providing him with this 'free and easy Oxford'.

Debating Society.

Chairman—Capt. Evans.
Secretary—Mr Angel.
Committee—Messrs Owen, Shaddick, Lee.

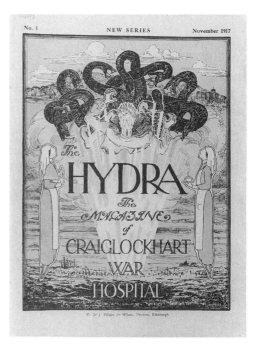

Left: Owen was editor of *The Hydra* from mid-July to September, when he announced that both the cover block and the editor were wearing out. Another patient, J.B. Salmond, took over as editor, with Owen as his assistant, and they reorganised the magazine during October. *Right*: The cover for the New Series, by Berrington, shows a patient battling with the hydra of shell-shock.

The Army authorities were more generous still, albeit wholly unintentionally, when they sent Siegfried Sassoon to Craiglockhart. Ergotherapy restored Owen to health and prepared him to take on new work, but it was Sassoon who revealed to him what that work should be.

Sassoon

Sassoon was admitted to the hospital on 23 July. Eight days later the place would have been buzzing with gossip, when readers of *The Times*

Siegfried Sassoon, a
portrait painted by Glyn
Philpot in June 1917.

discovered that he had just been argued about in the House of
Commons. He had been put away because he had circulated a
statement – quoted in *The Times* – accusing the Government of secretly
changing its war aims from 'defence and liberation' to 'aggression and
conquest'. He said that the original aims could now be achieved by
negotiation, adding that he was speaking on behalf of the troops, who
had no voice of their own. This extraordinary stand by a serving officer
could have been a grave embarrassment to the authorities and a boon
to the pacifists, who were demanding to know what the war was being
fought for and why negotiations could not be considered. The Under-
Secretary for War had been carefully briefed. He had been advised, he
said, that there must be 'something wrong' with this 'extremely gallant
officer'. He hoped honourable members would not exploit 'a young man
in such a state of mind'; if they did, their action would not be appreciated
by the officer's friends.

Sassoon was certainly under severe strain. His friends and fellow
officers had already intervened to get the whole affair hushed up; one of
them, Robert Graves, had persuaded him to obey orders and report to
Craiglockhart. Sassoon's decision not to pursue his protest was the

Robert Graves in November 1917.

beginning of a long humiliation. Bertrand Russell and the other pacifists who had secretly helped him thought he had abandoned the cause; he himself felt he had let down his comrades. He hated the hospital, calling it 'Dottyville' and suspecting that the 'drifting', 'haunted', 'degenerate-looking' patients were mostly shirkers. (His shame at being in such company suggests how Owen must have felt at first, with his own less 'gallant' record.) He used to say later that he could not have survived without the help of his doctor, W.H.R. Rivers.

Like Owen, Sassoon had dreamed of being a poet before the war and had written insubstantial lyrics in a nineties style. His war poetry had started as nobly sacrificial, then become increasingly realistic, until suddenly in 1916 he had begun producing satires, mostly aimed at the misleading language with which civilians – and sometimes soldiers – liked to clothe the realities of war.

> Home for ten days from that huge thunderstorm
>   Which blares and bellows doom beyond the Channel,
> He stretched his legs, contented, clean and warm,
>   Dressed in his old brown lazy suit of flannel.
> Patting the dog who rubbed against his knees,
>   He said, 'By Jingo, it's a glorious day!'
> Sunlight on garden-slopes and whispering trees
>   Made thirsty war seem strange and far away.
> 'O yes, we're doing fine!' (His wife was there
> Sitting beside him in a wicker chair.)
>   'I'm sure this summer'll see the fighting ended.'
> 'But, Jim, you said the same two years ago.'
> 'Well, things were rather rocky *then*, you know;
>   And we weren't *quite* so cheery as we pretended!'[8]

Owen probably read *The Times* report. He bought Sassoon's latest book, *The Old Huntsman and Other Poems*, and was intensely moved, not so much by the satires as by what he called the 'trench life sketches'. Looking back over his own experiences, he reckoned he had been a child until Beaumont Hamel. He sat up late writing his mother an emotional letter which may reflect his first reading of Sassoon. He said white men were in hell, sent there by civilization with the approval of the churches; as an officer, he was as guilty as anyone else. The notion that soldiers were Christs or avatars was 'a distorted view to hold in a general way'. 'I fear I've written like a converted Horatio Bottomley.' (Bottomley, the jingoistic editor of *John Bull*, often saluted Tommies as redeemers.)

On about 16 August Owen screwed up his courage and went upstairs to introduce himself. Sassoon was sitting on his bed cleaning golf clubs, the sun blazing on his purple dressing-gown. The social difference between himself and his visitor was immediately obvious. Sassoon was related to famous people, friendly with many more, and descended on his father's side from a fabulously wealthy dynasty. He had never

Sassoon's inscription in Owen's copy of *The Old Huntsman*, and a cutting which Owen slipped into the book.

needed to earn his living and had devoted much of his time before the war to hunting, cricket, and poetry. Standing nervously beside him, Owen produced some copies of *The Old Huntsman* and asked him to sign them.

Owen called again a few days later, and wrote excitedly to Gunston: 'He is very tall and stately, with a fine firm chisel'd (how's that?) head . . . After leaving him, I wrote something in Sassoon's style, which I may as well send you, since you ask for the latest.' The new poem was called 'The Dead-Beat'. It must have bewildered Gunston, who was used to thinking that poets should use words like 'chisel'd'. Sassoon believed in plain, contemporary language, truth to experience, and writing from the heart. 'The Dead-Beat' shows Owen already starting to absorb these

The Dead-Beat.   (True—in the incidental)

He dropped, more sullenly than wearily,
Became a lump of stench, a clot of meat,
And none of us could kick him to his feet.
He blinked at my revolver, blearily.

He didn't seem to know a war was on,
Or see or smell the bloody trench at all...
Perhaps he saw the crowd at Caxton Hall,
And that is why the fellows' pluck's all gone —

Not that the Kaiser frowns imperially.
He sees his wife, how coyly she chats;
And that his blue pal there, feeding fifty rats.
Hotels he sees, improved materially:

Where ministers smile ministerially.
Sees Punch still grinning at the Belcher bloke,
Bairnsfather, enlarging on his little joke,
While Belloc prophecies of last year, serially.

We sent him down at last, he seemed so bad,
Although a strongish chap and quite unhurt
Next day I heard the Doc's fat laugh. "That dirt
You sent me down last night's just died. So glad!"

The draft of 'The Dead-Beat' which Owen sent to Gunston on 22 August. His annus mirabilis begins with this poem.

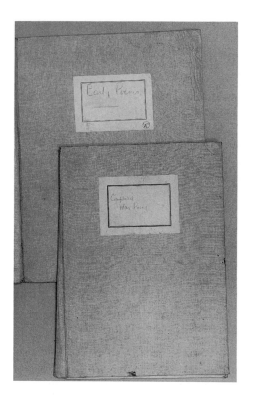

These folders, bought in Bordeaux, are probably the two 'khaki portfolios' which Owen asked his mother to extract from his desk in September 1917. He wrote the labels later: 'Early Poems' and 'Completed War Poems'.

principles; his great year had begun.

The new allegiance, as fervent as it was sudden, inevitably weakened an old one. Gunston was assembling a slim volume of verse, to be published at his own expense. Owen showed some of the poems to Sassoon, but Sassoon had rejected his own youthful style and could not now approve of imitation Swinburne. 'Sassoon considers E.L. Gunston not only flatulent, but hopeless', Owen wrote home. 'But he has not seen much of it.' 'He was appalled by Leslie's verbiage! I do think it a pity Leslie is in such a hurry.'[9] Owen sent copies of Sassoon's book to the two people he most wanted to convince, his father and cousin, saying it showed 'to the best possible advantage the tendencies of Modern Poetry'.

Sassoon was required to read Owen's work as well as Gunston's.

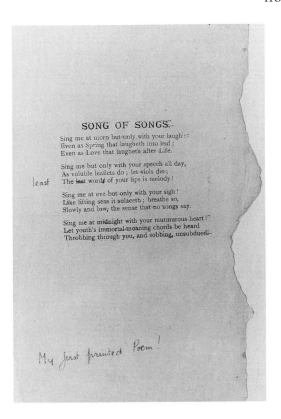

Hydra proof of 'Song of Songs', sent to Gunston with a comment.

Susan Owen had to break open a cupboard and send up hidden manuscripts. The new critic was not very interested; he thought Owen 'rather ordinary', and the poems seemed old-fashioned. Looking for something to praise, he picked out a recent lyric, 'Song of Songs', which used a system of rhymes he had never seen before. Owen published it anonymously in *The Hydra* on 1 September and was pleased to find it 'well received' by readers. Sassoon sent the magazine to friends, because his own 'Dreamers' was in the same number; he wrote under 'Song of Songs' in Lady Ottoline Morrell's copy: 'The man who wrote this brings me quantities & I have to say kind things. He will improve, I think!' He was too unhappy to notice much (his best friend had been killed on 15 August). 'The general expression of his face is one of boredom', Owen said. The way Sassoon looked over his visitor's head was exasperating, especially for a small man, but the new disciple was not to be deterred.

CRAIGLOCKHART WAR HOSPITAL,

SLATEFORD,

MIDLOTHIAN.

Six o'clock in Princes' Street.

In twos and threes, they have not far to roam,
Gray that Crowds eastward, gay of eyes;
Youths on their night out
Those seek no further than their quiet home,
Wives, that walk westward, slow and wise.

Neither should I go fooling over after clouds,
Following gleams unsafe, untrue,
And { pressing after { beauty through star-crowds,
{ tiring after
{ searching fastest | side by side
Dared I to walk along with you;

Or be you in the gutter where you stand,
Pale rain-flawed phantom of the place,
With news of all the nations in your hand,
And all their sorrows in your face.

'Six o'clock in Princes Street'. A lyric about the poetic impulse, influenced by Sassoon.

'Sweat your guts out'

By early September Sassoon and Owen had begun to be friends. Both were busy with new poems. Owen told his mother on 7 September that Sassoon had just called him in: 'having condemned some of my poems, and rejoiced over a few, he read me his very last works, which are superb beyond anything in his book'. Sassoon had been writing about shell-shock, as well as his own predicament:

> Do they matter? – those dreams from the pit? . . .
> You can drink and forget and be glad,
> And people won't say that you're mad;
> For they'll know that you've fought for your country
> And no one will worry a bit.
>
> ('Does it Matter?')

> I am banished from the patient men who fight.
> They smote my heart to pity, built my pride. . .
>
> The darkness tells how vainly I have striven
> To free them from the pit where they must dwell . . .
>   . . . Love drove me to rebel.
> Love drives me back to grope with them through hell;
> And in their tortured eyes I stand forgiven.
>
> ('Banishment')

Owen suggested some improvements and tried not to show how moved he was. He said that Sassoon was 'eminently *English*' in such matters, keeping 'all effusiveness strictly within his pages'. Yet as a friend Sassoon was 'intensely sympathetic, with me about every vital question on the planet or off it'. Their conversations provided the framework for much of what Owen was to write that autumn.

The nature of the war was one of the 'vital questions' the two poets must have talked about most often, although they avoided mentioning horrors. Sassoon did not know until years afterwards what Owen had gone through. It was enough to lend him Henri Barbusse's *Under Fire*, one of the most vivid denunciations of front line conditions so far published. That and Bertrand Russell's books, which Sassoon must also have recommended, gave Owen a new way of thinking about current

344

"Soldier's Dream".

I dreamed that Christ had fouled the big gun gears,
And made a permanent stoppage in all bolts,
And buckled with a smile, Mausers & Colts,
And rusted every bayonet with His tears.

And there were no more bombs, of ours or Theirs.
So we got out, and gathering up our plunder
Of wounds, and nightmares for the night, —
                                O wonder!
Leapt the Communication lines like flares!
A ~~bishop~~ ~~chaplain there, But there~~ Near home some bishops,
But there ~~crowded~~ priests a men of little sorrow,
~~Cried, Stay!~~, Ha!
~~Were they~~ Waylaid us saying, Ah! God's ways are most
                                mysterious.
I trust this move of His may not be serious,
And ~~that~~ pray new guns be issued you tomorrow."

We ~~passed~~ ~~him~~ ~~went on~~ til a man from U.S.A
Stopped us, and said " You go right back this
                                minute.
I'll follow. Christ! Your miracle ain't in it !
I'll those rifles mended by today.

Rough draft of 'Soldier's Dream'. Owen later dropped the Sassoonish stanza
about clergymen.

events. Many people who hated the war believed it had to be fought for the sake of a better world. If they were right, there was little point in drawing attention to trench realities. That was why Robert Graves disapproved of Sassoon's protest and 'corpse poems', arguing that they would merely weaken morale. Barbusse saw things differently: as a committed socialist, he thought the masses were being exploited by their rulers for imperial and commercial gain. Russell argued that the new world would be worse than the old, not better, because future thinkers and teachers were being destroyed; without their leadership, Europe would be prey to repression, violence, and social discontent. Owen was ready to respond to these ideas; he had said at the beginning of June that his 'Aim in War' was 'Extinction of Militarism *beginning* with Prussian'. Now he saw that the anger and disgust he had felt in France could be supported by reasoned argument.

There seemed no possibility that the war could be safely ended by military means, even though Lloyd George's coalition was committed to a 'fight to a finish'. The Passchendaele offensive was in progress, the worst of all the campaigns on the Western Front, and anyone who had been in the trenches could see through the relentless optimism of the newspapers. Negotiations seemed the only hope, yet the chance for them was fading. The High Command in Berlin was strengthening its power. If revolutionary Russia were to collapse, as seemed very likely, the Eastern Front would be overwhelmed in an immense German victory. Then would come the assault in the West. British politicians were urging the nation to hold on, because help was coming. A first detachment of American troops marched past the king in London on 15 August. Owen was pessimistic, writing gloomily at the end of the month of 'the Russians panicking, and getting out of the war, and ourselves getting deeper and deeper into it'. The arrival of the Americans seemed to mean that negotiations were even less likely, as he wrote in drafts of 'Soldier's Dream' in October:

> a General from out West
> Was shouting: Men! you go right back this minute.
> Well, Christ? I guess Your miracle ain't in it.
> I'll mend those guns. And see to Your arrest.

What could poets do? Listening to Sassoon, Owen thought of the Gunstons, Leslie composing patriotic verses and serving tea in

The two surviving drafts of 'Inspection', one of Owen's most Sassoonish poems. Both MSS were probably written at Craiglockhart.

Hampshire, Gordon soon to settle down as a married man, and their sister Dorothy writing letters full of noble sentiments. In Edinburgh people complained of the shortage of sugar and servants.[10] Sassoon believed that a poet's immediate duty was to make people see the truth.

245

Inspection.

" You! What d'you mean by this?" I rapped,
" You dare come on parade like this?"
" Please, sir, its—" " 'Old yer mouth," the sergeant snapped.
" I takes 'is name sir?" – " Please, and then dismiss."

Some days confined to camp he got,
For being dirty on parade.
He told me, afterwards, the damnèd spot
Was blood, his own. " Well, blood is dirt" I said.

" Bloods' dirt," he laughed, looking away, wound
To where in France Far off to where his body had bled,
And almost merged for ever into clay.
" The world is washing out its stains," he said.
It doesn't like our cheeks so red:
Young bloods its great objection.
But when we're duly white washed, being dead,
The race will bear Field-Marshall God's inspection."

Larger tasks would have to wait until peacetime, when the poets who
survived would be needed as guides, perhaps towards international co-
operation on the lines being advocated by H.G. Wells, with whom he
was in correspondence. Owen drafted some notes for a Wellsian play
about the future, perhaps hoping it would be suitable for a hospital
concert. It probably never got written. He was much too busy following
Sassoon's advice: 'Sweat your guts out writing poetry!'

Between his first attempt at 'The Dead-Beat' in August and his

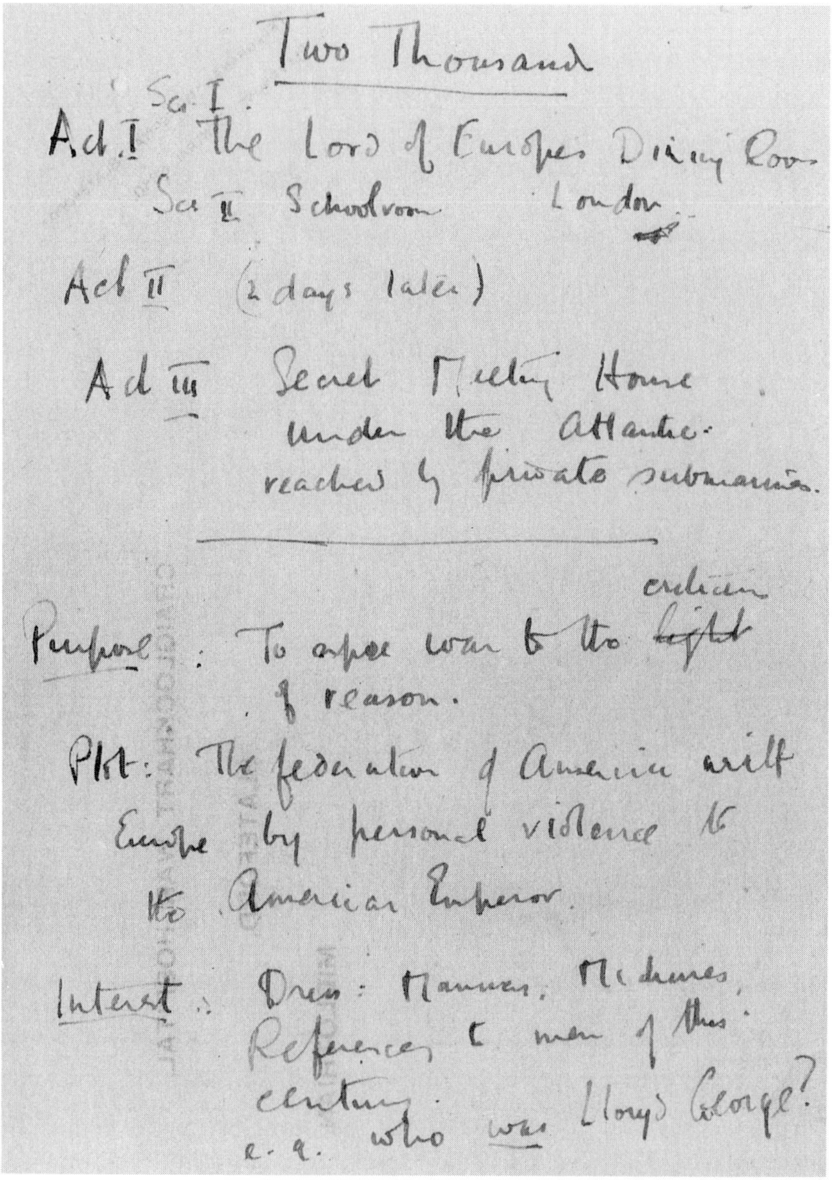

Two Thousand

Act.I Sc.I. The Lord of Europe's Dining Room
Sce II Schoolroom London.

Act II (2 days later)

Act III Secret Meeting House
under the Atlantic.
reached by private submarine.

Purpose: To expose war to the light of reason. *critician*

Plot: The federation of America will Europe by personal violence to its American Emperor.

Interest: Dress: Manners, Medicines, References to men of this century. e.g. who was Lloyd George?

'Two Thousand': a note for a play about the future. Written on the back of a sheet of Craiglockhart paper.

Anthem for Dead Youth.

What passing-bells for you who die in herds?
    - Only the ~~monstrous anger~~ ^{long monotony} of ~~the~~ guns!
to Only ~~the~~ stuttering rifles' rattled words
    Can patter out your hasty orisons, ~~pacing~~ hily
No wreaths for you, nor balms, nor ~~medals~~ ^{stately} choirs;
    Nor any ~~grievous crying~~ ^{voice of mourning}, save ^{our} of shells,
And bugles calling for you from your shires,
    Saddening the twilight. These are our farewells.

What candles may we hold to speed you all?
    ←-Not in the hands of boys, but in their eyes
Shall shine the ~~holy~~ lights of ~~long~~ ^{your} goodbyes.
The pallor of girls' brows must be your pall;
    Your flowers: the tenderness of ~~comrades'~~ ^{mortal} minds;
And each slow dusk, a drawing down of blinds.

                  Wilfred Owen.

This undated manuscript of 'Anthem for Dead Youth', sent to Gunston, is on a type of paper which Owen was using in late November–early December 1917. It is thus probably later than the other surviving complete drafts, all of which seem to be September–October. If the academic rules of editing are to be followed (as they probably never will be in this case), this version should be regarded as the final one.

discharge from hospital at the end of October, Owen drafted over a dozen poems. The first for which Sassoon could express heartfelt admiration was 'Anthem for Doomed Youth', written in September; he made a few amendments, eliminating some nationalistic implications – changing 'our guns' to 'the guns', for instance – and he tried to get it published. Then came 'Disabled', a description of a limbless casualty.

> He sat in a wheeled chair, waiting for dark,
> And shivered in his ghastly suit of grey,
> Legless, sewn short at elbow. Through the park
> Voices of boys rang saddening like a hymn, . . .

Graves was 'mightily impressed' with this poem when he came up on a visit in October; he thought Owen's work was 'too Sassoonish in places', but he saw more quickly than Sassoon did that Owen was 'the real thing', a genuine new talent.[11]

Most of Owen's 'Sassoonish' poems seem to have been begun at Craiglockhart. Perhaps the best-known is 'Dulce et Decorum Est', one of the most passionate and influential condemnations of war in English literature. Already he was able to write about his 'phantoms of the mind', making direct use of one of his worst nightmares. His advance was not quite so abrupt as it may appear; he had suffered from not dissimilar dreams for years before the war and had tried to describe them in verse. Now Brock had shown him how to control his phantoms

THE NEXT WAR.

*" War's a joke for me and you,
While we know such dreams are true."*—Sassoon.

Out there, we've walked quite friendly up to Death ;
  Sat down and eaten with him, cool and bland,—
Pardoned his spilling mess-tins in our hand.
We've sniffed the green thick odour of his breath,—
Our eyes wept, but our courage didn't writhe.
  He's spat at us with bullets and he's coughed
  Shrapnel. We chorussed when he sang aloft ;
We whistled while he shaved us with his scythe.

Oh, Death was never enemy of ours !
  We laughed at him, we leagued with him, old chum.
No soldier's paid to kick against his powers.
  We laughed, knowing that better men would come,
And greater wars : when each proud fighter brags
He wars on Death—for Life ; not men—for flags.

'The Next War', in *The Hydra*, 29 September 1917. The epigraph is from Sassoon's 'A Letter Home / (To Robert Graves)'.

The Chances   337

I mind as 'ow the night before the show
Us five got talkin', – we was in the know.
"Ah well!" says Jimmy, – an' 'e's seen some scrappin', –
"There's only one o' five things as can 'appen, –
Ye get a knock-out; nasty wound, or cushy;
Prisoner; or nowt except yer feelin' mushy."

          *   *   *

One of 'em's got the knock out, blown to chops.
One of 'em's wounded, loosin' both 'is props.
An' one, to use the word of 'ypocrites,
'Ad the misfortune to be took by Fritz.
Now me, I wasn't scratched, thank God Almighty,
– Though next time please, I'll thank 'im for a Blighty.
But poor young Jim, 'e's livin' an' 'e's not;
'E's killed and wounded, prisoner, all the lot.
'E reckoned 'e'd five chances, an' 'e 'ad
The bloody five all rolled in one. Jim's mad.

This is not the corrected version. but it will do.

A version of 'The Chances', probably written at Craiglockhart.

and Sassoon had shown him how to use them in the cause of peace. He had every reason to work flat out at writing. In his final *Hydra* he published a sonnet, 'The Next War', with an epigram from a poem addressed by Sassoon to Graves. They were his companions now

DULCE ET DECORUM EST

BENT double, like old beggars under sacks,
Knock-kneed, coughing like hags, we cursed through sludge,
Till on the haunting flares we turned our backs,
And towards our distant rest began to trudge.
Men marched asleep. Many had lost their boots,
But limped on, blood-shod. All went lame, all blind;
Drunk with fatigue; deaf even to the hoots
Of gas-shells dropping softly behind.

Gas! GAS! Quick, boys!—An ecstasy of fumbling
Fitting the clumsy helmets just in time,
But someone still was yelling out and stumbling
And flound'ring like a man in fire or lime.—
Dim through the misty panes and thick green light,
As under a green sea, I saw him drowning.

In all my dreams before my helpless sight
He plunges at me, guttering, choking, drowning.

If in some smothering dreams, you too could pace
Behind the wagon that we flung him in,
And watch the white eyes writhing in his face,
His hanging face, like a devil's sick of sin,
If you could hear, at every jolt, the blood
Come gargling from the froth-corrupted lungs
Bitten as the cud
Of vile, incurable sores on innocent tongues,—
My friend, you would not tell with such high zest
To children ardent for some desperate glory,
The old Lie: *Dulce et decorum est*
Pro patria mori.

'Dulce et Decorum Est', as printed in *Wilfred Owen: Poems* (1920), edited by
Sassoon and Edith Sitwell. Comparison with Owen's 'final' draft shows some of
the many pitfalls which his hasty amendments left for his editors.

through battle experience and poetry. He was not afraid any more.

He was discharged on 30 October, having been graded fit for light
duties. He was 'rather upset' to be 'rooted up from this pleasant Region'
and separated from Sassoon. There was an uproarious farewell party

In all your dreams, my friend, if you could pace
Behind the wagon that we flung him in,
And watch the white eyes writhing in his face,
His hanging face, like a devil's sick of sin;
If you could hear, at every jolt, the blood
Come gargling from the froth-corrupted lungs,
And think how once, his head was like a bud,
Obscene as 'cancer',
Fresh as a country rose, and keen, and young, —
You'd not repeat with such a noble zest,
To children ardent for some desperate glory,
The old Lie : Dulce et decorum est
Pro patria mori.

Of vile, incurable sores on innocent tongues
My friend, you would not tell with such high zest
To children

---

22 (2)

with his school class, and he apparently spent a few nights with the Grays. On the evening of 3 November, Sassoon met him for dinner at the Conservative Club in Princes Street, cheering up what might have been a miserable occasion by reading from a book of wonderfully bad verse which he had been sent by its author:

When Captain Cook first sniff'd the wattle,
When Love columbus'd Aristotle –
What gaudy-days in History![12]

The two friends disturbed the Club's usual hush with their helpless
laughter. When Sassoon said goodbye at the street door, he handed over
a sealed envelope. Owen sat on the stairs to open it, hoping he had been
entrusted with some great personal secret. He found a ten-pound note,
Robert Ross's address, and a brief message:

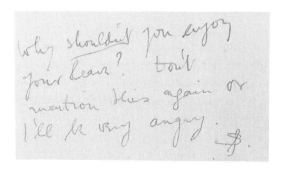

Owen 'groaned a little' at being tipped like a schoolboy, and went
upstairs to find a writing table, where he 'loosed off' a letter that was too
emotional to send. Then he walked over to Waverley Station and
caught the midnight train.

LIGHT DUTIES

'Oh! world you are making for me, Sassoon!'

OWEN had three weeks' leave after Craiglockhart. He began by going home, his first visit for nearly a year. 'I am spending happy enough days with my Mother,' he told Sassoon, 'but I can't get sociable with my Father without going back on myself over ten years of thought.' Tom Owen held strong conservative opinions and rarely saw eye to eye with his eldest son, but a verse he wrote in 1918 suggests he was less unsympathetic than he seemed.

> There was a young man in the Army,
> Who on poetry went slightly 'barmy';
> His odes on the War
> Were more telling by far
> Than all the proud boasts of the Army.

Being 'barmy', Owen probably spent hours at his desk, browsing among his books or looking out of his attic window at the familiar slopes of Haughmond Hill and the Wrekin beyond the Severn water meadows. He wrote to Sassoon on 5 November:

Know that since mid-September, when you still regarded me as a tiresome little knocker on your door, I held you as Keats + Christ + Elijah + my Colonel + my father-confessor + Amenophis IV in profile. . . . I love you, dispassionately, so much, so *very* much, dear Fellow, that the blasting little smile you wear on reading this can't hurt me in the least.

If you consider what the above Names have severally done for me, you will know what you are doing. And you have *fixed* my life – however short. You did not light me: I was always a mad comet; but you have fixed me. I spun round you a satellite for a month, but I shall

The Poetry Bookshop, 35 Devonshire (now Boswell) Street, Bloomsbury.

swing out soon, a dark star in the orbit where you will blaze.

Sassoon found that sort of thing embarrassing and later destroyed some even more outspoken letters. Yet it was one of Owen's strengths as a poet that his emotions were close to the surface, lacking the protective covering that might have been provided by a background like his friend's. He already knew that he was moving away into his own 'orbit' of originality, where his feelings could be given full expression.

He got away to London on 8 November, booking a room at the Regent Palace Hotel, just off Piccadilly Circus. His first call was at the Poetry Bookshop. Alida Klemataski, Harold Monro's friend and helper, was busy among the brightly coloured books and rhyme-sheets and recognized the visitor, much to his astonishment. Monro had been on anti-aircraft duty on Putney Heath and was now in hospital with fever. Hating the war, he and Alida were determined to keep the shop going as a beacon in darkness. Owen told her about Edinburgh and looked at the new books, probably buying Monro's latest volume, *Strange Meetings*.

Owen had followed Sassoon's advice by writing to Robert Ross, who invited him to lunch on 9 November amid the classical grandeur of the Reform Club in Pall Mall. They sat down at a table next to someone who

Alida Klemataski.

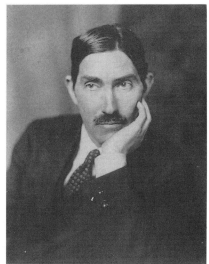

Harold Monro.

looked like 'an upstart rodent' but turned out to be Arnold Bennett. Another man joined them, his threatening eyes and huge moustache reminding Owen of bayonets seen over a sandbag, and Ross introduced H.G. Wells. The three club members often had lunch together, so the conversation was relaxed and the awed guest even managed to join in the banter. Over coffee, Wells kept Owen spellbound for an hour, telling him 'rare things' and 'a lot of secrets'. 'Little Owen went to see Robbie in town and made a very good impression', Sassoon told Graves later.[1]

Ross was well-known as an art dealer and connoisseur, and famous above all as Oscar Wilde's champion. With his big scarab ring and jade-green cigarette holder, he looked what he was, a figure from the nineties. He had an Aesthete's distaste for bourgeois attitudes and was privately scathing about the war. It was he who had encouraged Sassoon to write satires, although he deplored his protest. Painful experience had taught him the need for discretion. He had remained loyal to Wilde when other lovers and friends – including Wilde's favourite, Lord Alfred Douglas, – had proved false. After Wilde's death Douglas became a bitter enemy, waging a vicious campaign of public insults. He had no lack of evidence, but his quarry was protected by friendships at Downing Street until Asquith's fall at the end of 1916. Now Ross was vulnerable and knew it. His exquisite manners and

Robert Ross.

genial hospitality could not conceal the weariness of one who was waiting for a last, catastrophic attack.

Since 1914 Ross had lived in a first-floor flat at 40 Half Moon Street, Mayfair, under the care of the redoubtable Nellie Burton, formerly his mother's maid. Burton, as she was always called, ran the rest of the building as residential apartments. She knew all Ross's 'gentlemen' and liked to make a fuss of them, provided they behaved. (After the war, her lodgers included Sassoon's friends, Roderick Meiklejohn and Lord Berners, the musician, as well as some more obscure figures. When one young man shot himself in the bathroom to avoid scandal, Burton was not pleased: he should have done it in the park.) Sassoon was a special favourite; she would have been delighted to meet his young friend and apologetic that her rooms were full.

Ross asked Owen to dinner at the Club the day after they first met, and afterwards to Half Moon Street, where the talk went on until one in the morning. He was at home to friends every evening. It was taken for granted that most guests were, in the language of the time, 'so'. Owen met the most regular visitor, William More Adey, another former member of Wilde's inner circle. Now growing increasingly unkempt and eccentric, More Adey liked to pretend to be a dangerous anarchist.

Osbert Sitwell said he looked like a portrait of Lenin by Burne-Jones. In other respects the room had the splendour to be expected of Wilde's heir. It had recently been decorated in dull gold as a protest against war economies. Merely to enter it, Sassoon remembered, 'was a discovery of finely matured artistic judgement, for everything in it gave a sense of ripened and sensitive selection'. Owen was aware of old master paintings, antique bookcases, and a long table where biscuits, Turkish delight, brandy, and cigarettes were waiting. During the course of the evening, his poems were discussed with admiration. He came away full of new confidence and freedom: 'I and my work are a success'.

He went down to stay with Gunston at the YMCA hut, near Winchester, for a few days, stopping in London long enough to hear a concert at the Queen's Hall. Contemporary music had something in common with his new, discordant rhymes. Modern composers could hardly be expected to continue the sweet harmonies of the past. Gunston disagreed, of course. As they argued, Owen spoke more openly about his poems than he had ever done before, revealing a secret 'key' to many of them.[2] Presumably this included the information that the love poems were about boys, something that a friend of Ross could talk about at last. Gunston happened to be pursuing a new girlfriend. One way and another, he must have thought that his cousin had met some strange people since they had last seen each other.

Owen wrote a few days later, adding a postscript on the envelope which only came to light when Gunston unearthed it some sixty years later: 'I travelled up from Win: to Lond: with Bottomley. But didn't intrude on his Great Thoughts'. Two of the most influential writers on the war had been brought briefly face to face. The self-satisfied editor of *John Bull* ('The Paper on which the Sun Never Sets') probably took no notice of the unknown officer whose future fame would long outlast his own. A selection of Horatio Bottomley's 'Great Thoughts' had recently been published as a pocket anthology, and Owen knew the sort of thing the book contained:

> We have the men and the munitions; and it is death, death, death to the German, until – battered and broken, robbed of his arrogance, and stripped of his military stength – he asks for an armistice, and begs for Peace.

> The 'Conscientious Objector' is a fungus growth – a human toadstool – which should be uprooted without further delay.

If the God of Battles lives, then surely valour in a righteous cause is a passport to His presence! If somewhere beyond the bounds of time and space there is a Heavenly City, then surely our dead heroes are treading the pavements, erect, in the full glory of their splendid manhood – not dead, but the guests of God till we pass out into the light.

Owen looked out of the train window at the downs and could 'almost see' the dead again, lying about in the hollows, rotting into the autumn grass. It may even have been under the eye of the great journalist that he began drafting an answer to Bottomleyism: 'Asleep' seems to have been finished that day.

Pausing in London on his way back to Shrewsbury for the last few days of his leave, he spent an hour in the Poetry Bookshop. Monro was there this time, on convalescent leave. Owen felt obliged to ask about Gunston's book, which was due out any day, although Monro despised its vanity publishers. By a chance which seems almost symbolic, a

Asleep

Under his helmet, up against his pack,
After the so many days of work and waking
Sleep took him by the brow and laid him back.

There, in the happy no-time of his sleeping,
Death took him by the heart, There heaved a quaking
Of life, like child within him leaping,
Then chest and sleepy arms once more fell slack.

And soon the slow, stray blood came creeping
From the intruding lead, like ants on track.

Whether his deeper sleep lie shaded by the shaking
Of great wings, And the thoughts that hung the stars,
High-pillowed on calm pillows of God's making,
Above these clouds, these rains, these sleets of lead,
And these winds' scimitars,
—Or whether yet his thin and sodden head
Confuses more and more with the low mould,
His hair being one with the grey grass
Of finished fields, and wine-scraps rusty-old,
Who Knows? Who hopes? Who troubles? Let it pass!
He sleeps. He sleeps less tremulous, less cold,
Than we who wake, and waking say Alas!

Nov. 14. 1917.

'Asleep', sent to Gunston in Owen's letter of 16 November 1917.

parcel arrived and proved to contain Graves's new book, *Fairies and Fusiliers*. As Owen eagerly bought a copy and sat down on one of the rugged oak benches to leaf through it, he forgot the 'old song' that he and Gunston had loved to read and imitate. Graves's new work was enthralling. A customer started asking Monro who Sassoon was, and

Nov 16. 1917-

My dear Leslie,

I did not think to send back a driblet of your Ink so soon, but I have indeed carried off the key.
Has it been the key of my box I should surely have left it with you.
As it was I left you the key to many of my poems, which you will guard from rust or soilure.
As I said, if Hilda herself had any feeling for you, she would devise means of communication. I hope your plan succeeds.
Good of you to send me the lyric of Nov. 14th. I can only send my own of the same date, which came from Winchester Downs, as I crossed the long backs of the downs after leaving you. It is written as from the trenches. For I could almost see the dead lying about in the hollows of the downs.

I called at the Bookshop during my 3 hours in Town, & had a good chat with Monro, not forgetting to ask him about the Nymph. Graves' book had just came in while I was there. Haste thee, Nymph, and bring with thee Jest & youthful jollity! your W

Letter to Gunston, 16 November 1917.

Monro looked across at Owen and winked. Owen winked back. It was the sort of moment he loved: he was in the know, 'one of the ones', a poet's poet. He knew who to thank: 'Oh! world you are making for me, Sassoon!'

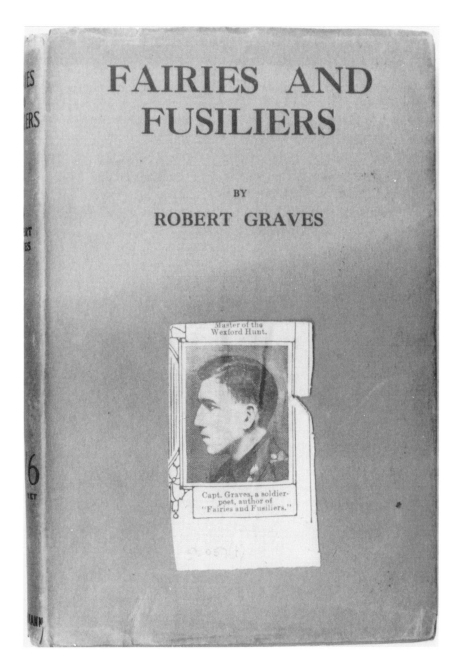

Owen's copy of *Fairies and Fusiliers*. He took the picture of Graves from a magazine and slipped it into the book.

The Clarence Gardens Hotel

Owen had trained with the 5th (Reserve) Battalion of his regiment, the Manchesters, in 1916 and was now ordered to join it in Scarborough. His journey lay through York, where he arrived at three in the morning on 24 November, hoping to spend the rest of the night in the Royal Station Hotel. Even the couches turned out to be full, and four dismal hours of knocking on other hotel doors brought no better result. He could use that sort of experience now. Remembering another dawn on the Somme, when the sense of being shut out had been far stronger, he would write in 'Exposure':

> Shutters and doors, all closed: on us the doors are closed, –
> We turn back to our dying.

He reported to the Northern Cavalry Barracks at Burniston, on the cliffs just north of Scarborough, only to find them occupied by the 'men', actually mostly boys, and NCOs. Some of the latter greeted him with respectful surprise, having heard he was dead. The officers, seventy or eighty of them, were quartered in the Clarence Gardens Hotel on the edge of the town. He recognized a few, including H.R. Bate. They told

Sunday morning Church Parade, North Bay, Scarborough, before the war. The Clarence Gardens Hotel, with its turret, stands at the end of the promenade. The barracks are on the cliffs beyond.

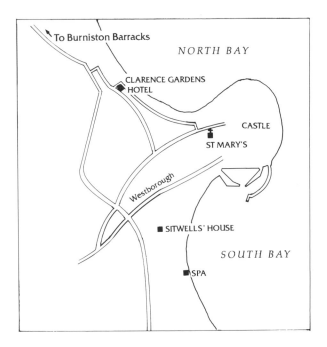

him life in the hotel was pleasant, except for the CO, a 'terrible old "Regular"'. Lieutenant-Colonel Mitchell was one of the Army's many 'dug-outs', old professionals excavated from retirement to take home commands in a war they did not understand. Having lost two sons at the front, he had no sympathy for 'neurasthenia'. He thought Owen a poor specimen and made his opinion obvious. Luckily some of the other officers were kindly. One or two had even read some 'war poetry'.

When Owen's letters were published in 1967, a footnote described him as 'Camp Commandant' at Scarborough. This annoyed Bate, who thought it too grand a title for a very junior job.[3] Owen was surprised, flustered, and perhaps none too flattered, to be put in immediate charge of the hotel's domestic arrangements.

I have to control the Household, which consists of some dozen Batmen, 4 Mess Orderlies, 4 Buglers, the Cook, (a fat woman of great skill,) two female kitcheners, and various charwomen!

They need driving. You should see me scooting the buglers round the dining-room on their knees with dustpan and brush! You should

Left: Enemy ships shelled Scarborough in December 1914, the first attack on the British mainland. The damage was extensively publicised as evidence of German barbarity.

Below: A 1915 postcard from Scarborough advertises the new bathing pool in the South Bay. Evidently holidaymakers had been scared away by rumours of further raids.

Scarborough's New Bathing Pool, Bungalows, Café &c &c right on the shore. It's all moonshine about Zeppelin Raids. Scarborough has never seen one

hear me rate the Charwoman for leaving the Lavatory-Basins unclean.

I am responsible for finding rooms for newcomers, which is a great

Owen's 'five-windowed turret' on the corner of the Clarence Gardens (now the Clifton) Hotel. He seems to have had the top room.

worry, as we are full up. This means however that I have a good room to myself, as well as my Office!

He was to lead some of those young orderlies into battle in 1918. The pressure of hotel business was exasperating at first. He had to get up at 6.30 a.m. to oversee breakfast, then deal with paperwork and order 'vast quantities of food'. Officers ate well, unlike other ranks. He was responsible for wine and tobacco, as well as for such duties as exercising prisoners and checking that the building showed no lights at night. The lack of time and the formal language needed for letters seemed likely to prove disastrous for poetry-writing.

After a while he began to realize he was lucky. The colonel was liable to explode if the bathwater was cold or the plates too hot, but he gave instructions that Owen could come and go at will and be excused parades. Having a room to oneself was a rare privilege. And such a room! It was another attic, with a ceiling so low in places that even a small man had to stoop, but in the far corner there was a turret-window, high above the sea, a perfect eyrie for a poet.[4] There was a comfortable bed and, best of all, a fire. It was impossible not to feel

North Bay and castle, Scarborough, from Owen's room.

hopeful. 'I *think* I am marked Permanent Home Service', he told his mother.

There were days that winter when the sun shone so dazzlingly that he half-closed the blinds and imagined he was back in the south of France. On other days there was nothing outside but fog, or the wind blew until the air was crystal-clear and the bay white with foam. 'I sit in the middle of my five-windowed turret, and look down upon the sea.' Like the Outlook Tower, it was a place for 'synoptic seeing'. The five windows commanded more than a half-circle, taking in the whole of the North Bay with its sandy beach and long respectable row of boarding houses curving round to the castle. At night, when dinner had been served and the kitchen cleared, the room was a secret haven. He moved his chair to the fire and settled down to read and write.

He read what he had brought with him or could find in the bookshops: Wells and Bennett, and a book about Wilde, representing his new London contacts; Barbusse, Stevenson, and Belloc, as a continuation of his Craiglockhart reading; two popular war poets, R.E. Vernède and Robert Service; John Masefield and W.W. Gibson, from among the Georgian group; and Graves and Robert Nichols, the two

Books read at Scarborough. Dec. 1917

R. Nichols : Ardours & Endurances
R. Graves : Fairies & Fusiliers
H. G. Wells : Stolen Bacillus
    "   : Wife of Sir Isaac Harman
H. Barbusse : Under Fire
W. Gibson : Battle
J. Masefield : Lollingdon Downs
                 Daffodil Fields.
Vernède   : War Poems
Stevenson : Dr. Jekyll & Mr. Hyde.
  Belloc :   Esto Perpetua.
Theocritus,
   Bion
   Moschus.
Robt Sherard : The Real O.W.
Arnold Bennett : The Regent
              "   ~~Art of War~~
R. W. Service -   Literary Taste
             passim.
Stopford Brooke : Studies in Poetry.

Owen's reading list for
December.

latest young poets to have caught the attention of reviewers. He had
bought Gibson's *Battle* in November, no doubt at the Poetry Bookshop,
where its author had been a founder-tenant; written in 1914–15, it was
a pioneering book, the first attempt by any English poet to describe
trench life as it really was. Sassoon had probably recommended it.
Owen had also bought the latest volume of Edward Marsh's anthology,
Georgian Poetry, published from the Bookshop; it contained work by
Sassoon, Graves, Nichols, Monro, Gibson, and Masefield. If he belonged
to any group, it was obviously this one. In Scarborough he bought a
translation of the Greek elegists[5] and set about studying the traditions of
classical and English elegy (a few months later he thought of publishing
his war poems as 'English Elegies').

One of the first posts at the hotel brought some copies of *The Nymph
and Other Poems* by E. Leslie Gunston. Owen read the book with a little of
the old enthusiasm and a lot of the new disapproval. 'I don't like "Hymn

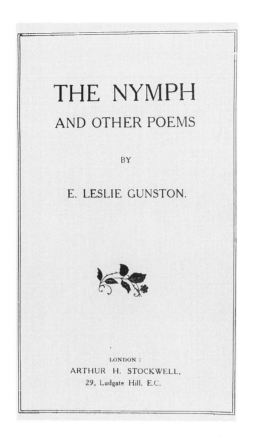

THE NYMPH

AND OTHER POEMS

BY

E. LESLIE GUNSTON.

LONDON :
ARTHUR H. STOCKWELL,
29, Ludgate Hill, E.C.

TO
WILFRED OWEN
I DEDICATE
THIS BOOK
WITH AFFECTION.

Gunston's book: title page and dedication.

of Love to England", naturally, at the period while I am composing "Hymns of Hate"'. He wrote to Gunston as kindly as he could, but in letters home he gave his frank opinion.

> Concerning Leslie's book, I may say privately that it is a mere orgy of kissing, and does nobody any good.
> Were these poems founded on a single act or fact they might have been written to some poetic purpose and value. But that is not so, which is no doubt the more admirable from a *Pauline* point of view, but the more pitiable in a *human* aspect. Nothing great was said of anything but a definite experience.[6]

Sassoon could have put it no better. Owen sent him a copy of *The*

Nymph, later reporting to Gunston that there had been no response and adding that for Sassoon poetry had become 'a mere vehicle of propaganda'. If that was an admission that Sassoon's work was not all that a poet should aim for, Graves would have agreed. He told both Owen and Sassoon to 'cheer up': 'a poet should have a spirit above wars'.[7] Owen set out his own view in 'Apologia pro Poemate Meo', denying the value of his cousin's 'old song', accepting Graves's point that a poet's spirit should rise 'Past the entanglement' of the battlefield, and insisting, with Sassoon, that no civilian should be enabled to share the secret love and beauty which only soldiers knew.

> You shall not hear their mirth:
> You shall not come to think them well content
> By any jest of mine. These men are worth
> Your tears. You are not worth their merriment.

Sassoon had actually more or less given up 'propaganda'. He had been told he could return to duty if he promised to keep quiet. Owen tried to dissuade him with a Shelleyan poem, urging him to fight for truth, not war.

> Earth's wheels run oiled with blood. Forget we that.
> Let us turn back to beauty and to thought . . .

Sassoon was not convinced. He left Craiglockhart in late November, rejoining his regiment on 11 December.

Owen revisited Edinburgh just before Christmas, the boys at Tynecastle School having reminded him of a promise to spend some of his first leave with them. Once again he breakfasted at the North British Hotel and set out for Craiglockhart. Dr Brock greeted him appropriately with one word, 'Antaeus!' He meant that Owen's poem was wanted for *The Hydra*. Other greetings were less welcome, staff and inmates assuming that the former patient had suffered a relapse. The school, by contrast, was exhilarating. His name was on the blackboard, because the boys were composing Christmas letters to him; they gave him his present, a hundred cigarettes, and carried him off to play in Minnehaha's wigwam. He could have stayed at St Bernard's Crescent, but preferred to dine there and find lodgings. He returned to Scarborough in time for Christmas, which was enlivened by an

The Unsaid   279

I, too, saw God through mud,
The ~~& mud~~ that cracks on cheeks when wretches smile,
~~And, foul~~ ~~I found saw~~
~~And~~ more glory ~~the~~ in their eyes than blood,
~~And in~~ their laughs more glee ~~than shakes~~ a child.
And glee, that almost made its gloom worth while.
                dropped
I also have ~~left~~ fear
Behind the barrage, dead as my platoon
~~And~~ And smiled ~~of joyful shipct~~ ~~& light~~ and clear
         felt of shrill safely,
Past the ~~iron~~ tar entanglement where my hopes were strewn.
                                  lone seen
          witnessed
I ~~have~~ ~~seen~~ exultation:
Faces that ~~were obscene~~ used to curse me, scowl for scowl.
                                      with
Let ~~Bloys~~ shine and ~~soft~~ lifted ~~with~~ divine passion of oblation
Seraphic for an hour; though they were foul.

I have made fellowships
Not told of ~~mortal~~ lover in ~~his~~ song,
For love is not the binding of your lips
~~With~~ silk soft silk of eyes that look and long.
In

Draft work for 'Apologia pro Poemate Meo', probably written at Clarence Gardens, November–December 1917.

Athenaeum
Aug. 13, 1920

Poetry

FRAGMENT

Earth's wheels run oiled with blood. Forget we that,
Let us turn back to beauty and to thought.
Better break ranks than trek away from progress.
Let us forgo men's minds that are brute natures,
Let us not sup on blood which some say nurtures,
Be we not swift with swiftness of the tigress.

Beauty is yours, and you have mastery;
Wisdom is mine, and I have mystery;
We two will stay behind and keep our troth.

Miss we the march of this retreating world
Into vain citadels that are not walled.
Let us lie out and hold the open truth.

Then when their blood has clogged the chariot wheels
We will go up and wash them from deep wells,
Even the wells we dug too deep for war.

For now we sink from men as pitchers falling,
But men shall raise us up to be their filling,
The same whose faces bled where no wounds were.

WILFRED OWEN.

[Wilfred Owen was killed in action on Nov. 4, 1918.]

'Earth's wheels': a cutting annotated by Edmund Blunden. One of Owen's least-known poems, this seems to be the exhortation to keep out of the war which he sent to Sassoon in November. Editors have always treated it as a fragment, or as draft work for 'Strange Meeting', but it is in fact a complete poem.

encouraging letter from Graves and 'crowds' of cards, and blighted by a nasty display of Colonel Mitchell's temper.

At the 'intolerable instant' when 1917 gave way to 1918, Owen was in his room, no doubt in his fleecy dressing-gown and purple slippers in front of the fire. From beyond the turret came the sound of the sea. He was writing to his mother, reviewing the year in the old evangelical way she had taught him as a child, and counting his blessings. There was one above all: 'I go out of this year a Poet, my dear Mother, as which I did not enter it. I am held peer by the Georgians; I am a poet's poet.' He was clear about his subject and, at that intolerable instant, his future.

> 30/12/17
>
> 5th (Res.) Battn. MANCHESTER REGT.,
> CLARENCE GARDENS,
> SCARBOROUGH.
>
> My dear Leslie,
> It is overlong since I wrote ; but now, composed by the my bedroom fire this Sunday afternoon , my thoughts impel themselves after you, I wish you were here to read a little Swinburne, whom I find particularly fine on Sundays. Have you yet got Gosse's Life of A.C.S.? I had a longish letter from Sassoon recently, saying he will

Part of a letter to Gunston, 30 December 1917.

He remembered the troops at Etaples a year before and the look on their faces:

> It was not despair or terror, it was more terrible than terror, for it was a blindfold look, and without expression, like a dead rabbit's.
>
> It will never be painted, and no actor will ever seize it. And to describe it, I think I must go back and be with them.

'Held peer by the Georgians'

Owen entered 1918 determined to consolidate his new-found status as a recognized poet. When hotel affairs swallowed a whole day, as they sometimes did, he resented the loss of time:

> on such days I have no time to settle down to my art. For it is an art, & will need the closest industry. Consider that I spend – what? – three hours a week at it, which means one fruitful half-hour, when I ought to be doing SIX hours a day by all precedents.

War pervaded everything. His batman was a bad case of shell-shock in need of a rest, and the possible substitute, 'a secondary-school-educated youth', had a leg wound and was still wearing 'shell-torn' boots. Scurrying up and down the hotel stairs affected his own left foot, which had never quite recovered from frost and rain on the Somme. At least that gave him an excuse to keep to his room and his real 'job', his 'duty'. 'I confess I *bring on* what few war dreams I now have, entirely by *willingly* considering war of an evening. I do so because I have my duty to perform towards War.' He still remembered Brock's teaching: dreams could be controlled and used through effort and will. It was dangerous work.

The fire in the turret-room smoked 'horribly' when the wind blew, providing 'the right atmosphere' for war poems. The embers glowing at night like 'crusted dark-red jewels' were useful for 'Exposure'. He may have been sitting by the fire, on 13 or 14 January, when he read newspaper reports of a disastrous colliery explosion in Staffordshire; the sound of the coals combined with the stories of men and boys lost underground to give him the idea for 'Miners'. He wrote the poem in half an hour and sent it to *The Nation*, which had published Sassoon and other Georgians. It came out a fortnight later, earning him two guineas, one of which he sent home to be spent on fires ('only poetic justice. Stoke up!'). 'Miners' was the first of his poems to be published, except for the two he had included anonymously in *The Hydra*.

Gunston complained that the rhymes in 'Miners' offended his 'musical ear', and he expressed doubts about Graves and Sassoon. In reply, Owen warned him not to make himself 'a lagoon, salved from the ebbing tide of the Victorian age', and offered to lend him *Georgian Poetry*.

Poetry.

MINERS.

THERE was a whispering in my hearth,
  A sigh of the coal,
Grown wistful of a former earth
  It might recall.

I listened for a tale of leaves
  And smothered ferns,
Frond-forests, and the low sly lives
  Before the fawns.

My fire might show steam-phantoms simmer
  From Time's old cauldron,
Before the birds made nests in summer,
  Or men had children.

But the coals were murmuring of their mine,
  And moans down there
Of boys that slept wry sleep, and men
  Writhing for air.

I saw white bones in the cinder-shard,
  Bones without number.
For many hearts with coal are charred,
  And few remember.

I thought of all that worked dark pits
  Of war, and died
Digging the rock where Death reputes
  Peace lies indeed:

Comforted years will sit soft-chaired,
  In rooms of amber,
The years will stretch their hands, well-cheered
  By our life's ember;

The centuries will burn rich loads
  With which we groaned,
Whose warmth shall lull their dreaming lids,
  While songs are crooned;
But they will not dream of us poor lads
  Lost in the ground.

                WILFRED OWEN.

'Miners', published in *The Nation*, 26 January 1918.

Jan. 8. 1918

My dear Leslie,

I was glad to find you take up a strong attitude with regard to your poetry & mine.

You ask me if I saw the Reviews of S.S. I have read every word of them — in his huge book of Press Cuttings. The vast majority are entirely appreciative. As for Graves, have you seen Chambers' Journal lately, or the Sat. Westminster? (And remember the Edinburgh Review: fame itself!

Letter to Gunston, 8 January, defending Sassoon and Graves.

Poor Gunston had brought out *The Nymph* with all the excitement of a new author. His rewards were one small review, which said he lacked originality and power, and an abrupt end to the encouragement which had kept him going since his cousin had first got him interested in poetry five years earlier. He defended himself, but he never published another book.

It was as a Georgian that Owen accepted an invitation to Graves's wedding on 23 January. 'It is a kind of duty both to myself and Graves to

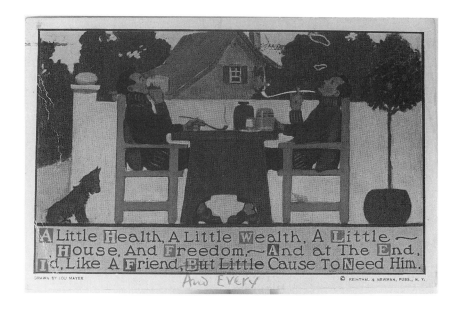

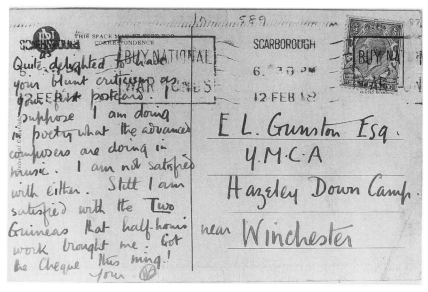

Postcard to Gunston, 12 February, responding to some 'blunt criticism' of the sound-effects in 'Miners'.

Nancy Nicholson, in landgirl's costume, and Robert Graves. Wales, June 1918.

go', he told his mother, knowing she would be hurt by his once again taking leave for something other than a visit home. He placated her by spending the night of 22 January at Shrewsbury, although it meant catching an early train next day. Arriving at Paddington, he hired a bathroom in the hotel, just had time for a shave, and was about to get into the bath when his taxi was announced. He said afterwards that he got to the Reform 'punctually' for lunch with Ross, but Ross might not have agreed; they had to leave in a hurry, exchanging a few words with Wells on the way, and hailed a cab for the short journey to St James's, Piccadilly.

It was a fashionable church, but not a fashionable wedding. Some of the guests looked positively dowdy, Owen thought. He was disappointed not to see Sassoon, who disapproved of the marriage and had stayed away. Graves was nervous but calm, wearing full uniform with spurs and sword. The bride, Nancy Nicholson, was secretly furious, having just discovered what she was required to swear to. At the reception, which was held at her father's flat in Apple Tree Yard nearby, she grabbed a bottle of champagne and went off to change into her

Letter from Robert Graves, 1 February, thanking Owen for a wedding present of eleven apostle spoons. Owen explained at the wedding that the missing twelfth spoon had been court-martialled for cowardice and was awaiting execution.

landgirl's costume. Owen was delighted to be introduced to people as 'Owen, the poet'; he talked to a pleasant gentleman who he later realized was Edward Marsh, and a handsome, rather serious young

a most awfully good person — I
see no prospect of tiring of her for
quite a little time.

for a month

Tomorrow she goes back to her
farm, I to my fusiliers — Then I'll
be able to think again — Lately I've
been quite off my head — I may
even write poetry, who knows?

Well, it was ripping of you to
give us that present & splendid
to come all that way to the
wedding. God reward you.

Write more poetry.
I hope you found Marsh & Scott Moncrieff
worth talking to

Yours ever
Robert Graves.

Scottish officer named Scott Moncrieff, who had been badly lamed on
the Somme. They were two of Graves's most helpful advisers on verse
matters. Graves's two publishers, Monro and Heinemann, had also
been invited.

In the evening Owen dined again at the Reform, this time with
Roderick Meiklejohn, whom he afterwards discovered to be a senior
civil servant and former private secretary to Asquith. Meiklejohn had

Charles Scott Moncrieff.

visited Sassoon at Craiglockhart and was a faithful friend, although Sassoon used to find his company 'slightly dreary', like 'talking to the family solicitor'.[8] After dinner they went to Half Moon Street, where they found Ross and 'two Critics', Charles Scott Moncrieff and probably More Adey. Scott Moncrieff wrote about Owen later.

> It was in January, 1918, at the crowded wedding of another poet, that I first saw him. I had been provisionally released from hospital a few days earlier, and had spent all that day, ineffectively, at a Police Court. I was too sore at first, in mind and body, to regard very closely the quiet little person who stood beside me in a room from which I longed only to escape. But that evening I met him again after dinner, and found that we had already become, in some way, intimate friends.[9]

The trial at which Scott Moncrieff had apparently been giving evidence must have been that of his much more intimate friend, Christopher Millard, who was about to be jailed for a homosexual offence. Millard was Wilde's bibliographer and Ross's former secretary; his fate must have been a topic for worried discussion that evening, certain as it was to provide ammunition for Ross's enemies.

Delighted to find a new companion, Scott Moncrieff engaged Owen in earnest, literary talk. His own war poems were conventional and heroic; he disliked Sassoon's and may have been partly responsible for Graves's doubts about them, so he would have had reservations about Owen's, had it not been for pararhyme. He was hoping to enliven his convalescence by translating the *Song of Roland* into English verse and was puzzling over what to do with the old French assonances. Such problems always fascinated him (later he was to become famous as the translator of Proust and other difficult texts). The rhymes in 'Miners' seemed a brilliant solution. Owen knew the *Song of Roland* and revealed an impressive mastery of French. Scott Moncrieff's enthusiasm was flattering, perhaps not less so because it was evidently not confined to matters of scholarship. The gathering did not break up until two in the morning. By the time Owen left for his hotel room – at the Imperial in Russell Square this time – it was agreed that Ross should 'ruminate' over his poems with a view to advising on publication.

Three days later the attack on the 'Oscar Wilde cult' began. A right-wing newspaper owned by an eccentric MP called Pemberton Billing alleged that the German Secret Service had a 'Black Book' which listed the names of 47,000 eminent British people whose sexual tastes were questionable. The public seized on this ludicrous story as a welcome diversion from news of the stalemate at the front. Lord Alfred Douglas had been given his opportunity.

Friends, oysters, antique-shops

The pleasures of a near-civilian life in Scarborough increased in February when a disagreeable mess president was replaced by Lieutenant Priestley, a tall, good-natured man whom everyone called 'Uncle Henry'.[10] He and Owen had already become friendly, finding that they shared an interest in antique furniture, and had started making expeditions to shops and sale rooms. Owen was dreaming of finding a cottage after the war. His purchases eventually included a table, a chest of drawers, some tall candlesticks, and probably a little bronze of Hermes. Buying for the future was a way of defying war.

Owen had to work closely with Priestley, and Bate noticed him only as 'Priestley's shadow', sheltering from the wrath of the colonel and

St Mary's Church and an alley in
the old town, Scarborough.

never exchanging a word or smile with anyone else. He seemed either
painfully shy or insufferably arrogant. Bate was to allow him the benefit
of the doubt until he read the *Collected Letters* fifty years later, when their
repeated references to other officers as '"temporary" gentlemen'
convinced him that snobbery had been the reason for Owen's aloofness.
There was some truth in that. For one who had progressed from gloomy
Birkenhead to Ross's golden room, conversation and bridge in the
crowded hotel lounges held no great attraction.

Despite wanting to spend long hours working in his solitary turret,
Owen was not entirely unsociable. One of his family's favourite
relations, 'Cousin May', ran a school in Scarborough, and he visited her.
One of her friends gave him some more German lessons. There was also
a painter called Claus, apparently a Belgian refugee and counter-spy,
who knew and revered Ross; he and Owen spent an evening getting
'drunk' on the picturesque alleys of the old town. Another new
acquaintance, Philip Bainbrigge, also belonged to Ross's world. He was
Scott Moncrieff's closest friend, a tall, short-sighted figure who looked
more like the schoolmaster he had been than the subaltern in the
Lancashire Fusiliers his uniform proclaimed him to be. Once again

331

He looked down, from the great height of death,

"Having forgotten ~~what~~ ~~he~~ ~~was~~ ~~why~~:
how he died, and why;

~~And saw this planet~~

~~His~~ ~~continent~~ ~~craters like the moon~~
changing

~~And pitted with the pock marks of~~ slack
pocks

~~And he sees~~ the ~~long plain~~ grey and ~~black~~ with
earth's face   shrunk   dearth
                                                cruel
And ~~to~~ pitted like   with hollow
    ~~craters like~~ ~~the~~ ~~moon's~~   woe,
All pitted with pocks that
              great   ~~of~~ ~~his~~ ~~disease.~~
                                    some old   shame.
                                    her disease.
                                    ~~And~~ ~~disgrace.~~
                          and scabs of plague.

cold
~~it called~~
sweat   ~~It seemed that caterpillars~~
swart   And caterpillars crawled and swarmed and
                                              and   curled
                Thousands on thousands, ~~till these~~ fling
                The ditches, ~~and the wrinkles and~~ killed,
                                                    they break up;

death   ~~And others caterpillars,~~ and break up,
dearth   where they writhe,
that   ~~And~~ ~~other~~   creepers   swarm the
thought   But long slow bristly creatures come yet more
                                              some brownish;
                ~~Some~~ ~~brown~~; ~~some~~ blue, some grey   may
                    and green; some ~~of~~ blue, some grey.

                And as it seems the grey
                    now the blue eats up
                ~~And all the grey~~   the
                Leaving the green parts, ~~of the earth~~ for mud,
                And those live creatures that were grey
                ~~Have~~ ~~was~~ upon the rest, and dro
                    warred with the rest, and eat the
                                              and were we
                                                  eaten.

Owen found himself on easy terms with a public school man. Sassoon was Marlborough and Cambridge, Graves Charterhouse and destined for Oxford, Scott Moncrieff Winchester and Edinburgh; Bainbrigge was not only Eton and Cambridge, but also a former master at Shrewsbury School, an institution Owen had often gazed at with envy and regret.

Bainbrigge was formidably learned and very entertaining. He had a talent for light verse 'of a private kind'; hidden away in research libraries there are still a few of the obscene rhymes he and Scott Moncrieff wrote for each other's amusement, full of secret jokes and erudition. Bainbrigge's attitude to the war was refreshingly unsoldierly; he hoped he would not be remembered as a hero but as a lover of 'good dinners, curious parody, / Swimming, and lying naked in the sun', the intricacies of classical literature, and 'Beethoven, Botticelli, beer, and boys'.[11]

Owen himself made an incautious mention of '*mon petit ami* in Scarboro'' in a letter to Gunston. He usually found a boy or two to befriend, wherever he was, probably more often than his letters reveal. These relationships could be presented as innocent or romantic, depending on the company present. It was perhaps with Bainbrigge's encouragement in February that he composed three 'curious' ballads. Two of them now make little sense, but there was presumably a 'key' which could be told to friends. The third is simple enough:

> Nay, light me no fire tonight,
>   Page Eglantine;
> I have no desire tonight
>   To drink or dine;
> I will suck no briar tonight,
>   Nor read no line;
> An you be my quire tonight,
>   And you my wine.

A better-known poem of this period begins

> I am the ghost of Shadwell Stair.
>   Along the wharves by the water-house,
>   And through the cavernous slaughter-house,
> I am the shadow that walks there.

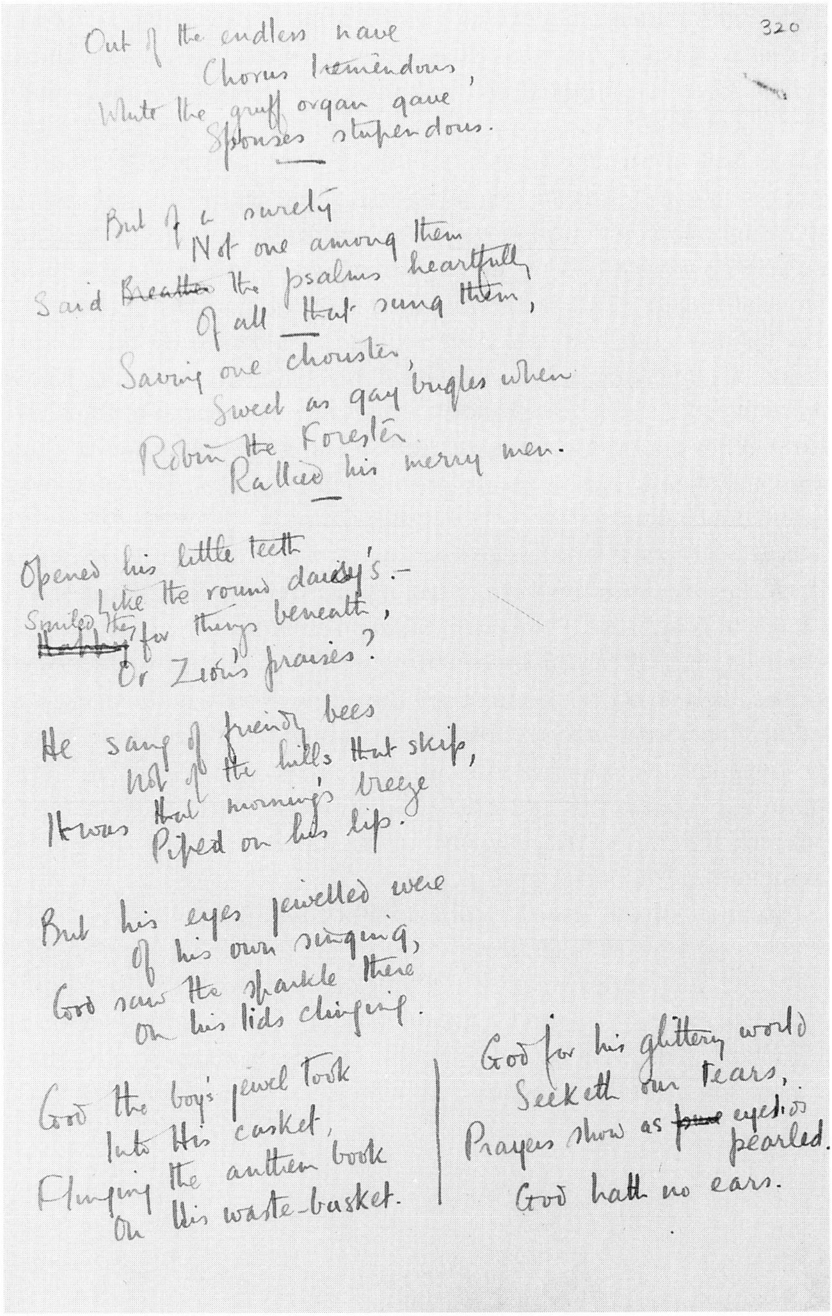

320

Out of the endless nave
Chorus tremendous,
While the gruff organ gave
Sponses stupendous.

But of a surety
Not one among them
Said Breathes the psalms heartfully
Of all that sung them,
Saving one chorister,
Sweet as gay bugles when
Robin the Forester
Rallied his merry men.

Opened his little teeth
Like the round daisy's –
Smiled they for things beneath,
Or Zion's praises?

He sang of friendly bees
Not of the hills that skip,
It was that morning's breeze
Piped on his lip.

But his eyes jewelled were
Of his own singing,
God saw the sparkle there
On his lids clinging.

God the boy's jewel took
Into His casket,
Flinging the anthem book
On his waste-basket.

God for his glittery world
Seeketh our tears,
Prayers show as eyes so pearled.
God hath no ears.

Draft of 'A Tear Song', a poem in Wilde's manner.

Scott Moncrieff was shown this poem and he left a partial 'key' to it, suggesting that the ghost was Owen himself, lingering in the East End at night.[12] Owen certainly seems to have known the area; there really were a waterworks and a slaughter-house near Shadwell Dock Stair.

This sort of writing was in the Wilde tradition, which required initiates to come very close to revealing the truth without saying anything that would arouse more than a vague unease in the minds of people who were not in the know. Owen's attempts at the convention were not unsuccessful, if the unease of some of his modern commentators is any guide. He had been studying Wilde during the winter, reading *De Profundis* and biographies. Possibly life in Scarborough was beginning to distract him from his 'duty' as a war poet. On the other hand, Wilde had been a fighter, like Sassoon, satirizing middle-class complacency and speaking out for voiceless prisoners. That, too, was part of the tradition.

On 22 February Bainbrigge and Owen met in the little oyster bar which they and Priestley frequented, and viewed the state of the world with gloom. At home, Pemberton Billing's newspaper had just given a new twist to the Black Book story by pointing to a private production of Wilde's *Salome*, as an example of the wickedness endangering the nation. It was obvious that Ross's name would be dragged in. Abroad, the Germans were completing their massive victory in the east. Bainbrigge 'opined that the whole of civilization is extremely liable to collapse'. If the expected happened on the Western Front, all reserves would be needed.

Owen had already heard that he might be sent to a command depot, 'which is where most Light Duty Officers "end up", doing physical drill, to fit them for serious warfare'. Orders came through that he should report to Ripon on 12 March. 'An awful Camp', he lamented as soon as he arrived. 'Farewell Books, Sonnets, Letters, friends, fires, oysters, antique-shops. Training again!'[13]

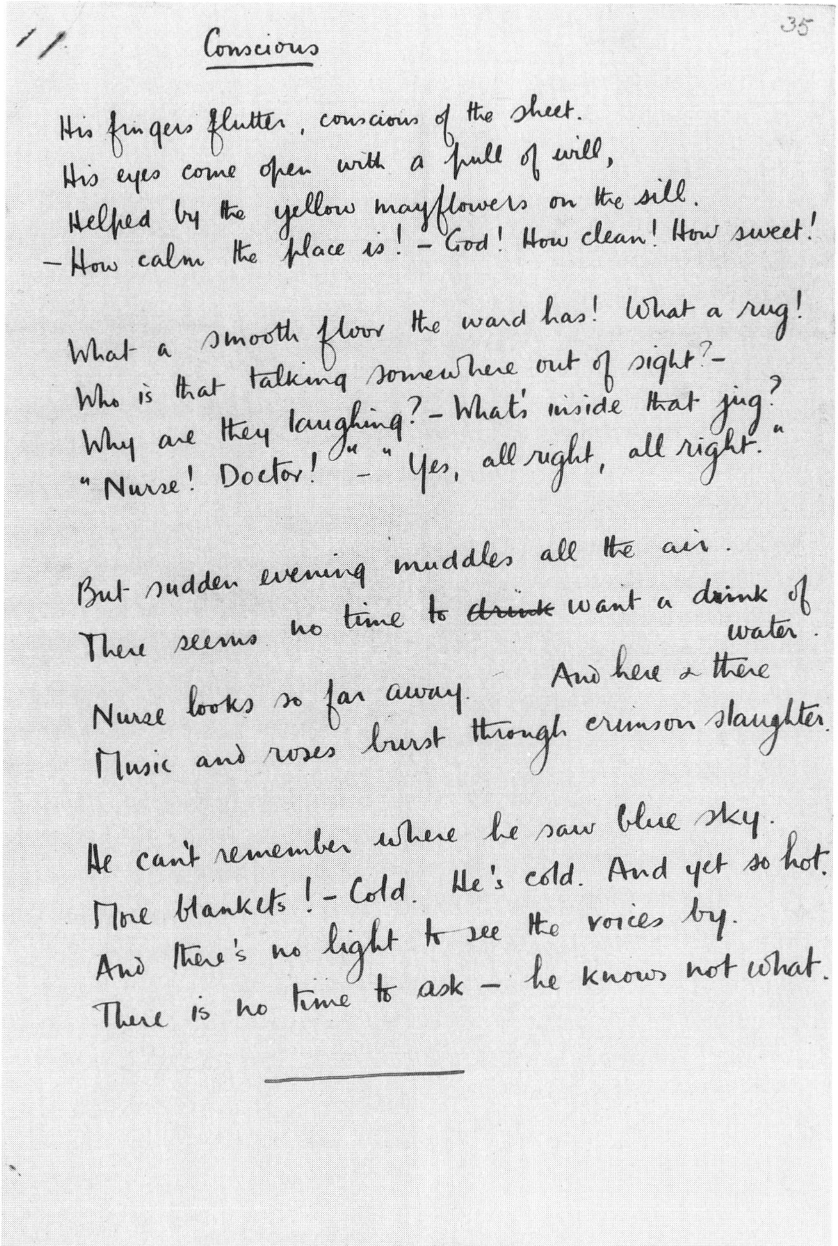

/ /.

35

Conscious

His fingers flutter, conscious of the sheet.
His eyes come open with a pull of will,
Helped by the yellow mayflowers on the sill.
— How calm the place is! — God! How clean! How sweet!

What a smooth floor the ward has! What a rug!
Who is that talking somewhere out of sight? —
Why are they laughing? — What's inside that jug?
"Nurse! Doctor!" — "Yes, all right, all right."

But sudden evening muddles all the air.
There seems no time to ~~drink~~ want a drink of
water.
Nurse looks so far away.   And here & there
Music and roses burst through crimson slaughter.

He can't remember where he saw blue sky.
More blankets! — Cold. He's cold. And yet so hot.
And there's no light to see the voices by.
There is no time to ask — he knows not what.

_____

One of the three known drafts of 'Conscious'. Owen worked on this poem at Scarborough.

40

Wild with all Regrets.
[To S·S.] *

My arms have mutinied against me, — brutes!
My fingers fidget like ten idle brats.
My back's been stiff for hours, damned hours.
Death never gives his squad a stand at ease.
I can't read. There, it's no use. Take your book.
A short life and a merry one, my buck!
We said we'd hate to grow dead-old. But now,
Not to live old seems awful: ~~Not~~ not to renew
My boyhood with my boys, and teach 'em
Shooting and hunting, — all the arts of ~~hurting~~ hitting.
— Well, that's what I learnt, — That, and making money.
Your fifty years in store seem none too many,
But I've five minutes. God! For just two years
To help myself to this good air of yours!
One Spring! Is one too hard to share? Too long?
Spring air would find its own way to my lung,
And grow me legs as quick as lilac-shoots.

x   x   x

* May I?

One of the poems Owen wrote by his fire at Clarence Gardens. 'Wild with all
Regrets' was later revised as 'A Terre'.

41

Yes, there's the orderly. He'll change the sheets
When I'm lugged out. Oh, could'nt I do that?
Here in this coffin of a bed, I've thought
I'd like to kneel and sweep his floors for ever, —
And ask no nights off when the bustle's over,
For I'd enjoy the dirt. Who's prejudiced
Against a grimed hand when his own's quite dust,
—Less live than specks that in the sun-shafts turn?
Dear dust — in rooms, on roads, on faces' tan!
I'd love to be a sweep's boy, black as Town;
Yes, or a muck-man. Must I be his load?
A flea would do. If one chap wasn't bloody,
Or went stone-cold, I find another body.

                    ×   ×   ×

Which I shan't manage now. — Unless its yours.
I shall stay in you, friend, for some few hours.
You'll feel my heavy spirit chill your chest,
And climb your throat on sobs, until its chased
On sighs, and wiped from off your lips by
                                        wind.

I think on your rich breathing, brother, I'll be weaned
To do without what blood remained me from my
                                        wound.

Dec. 5. 1917

— 4 —

TRAINING AGAIN

Ripon

THE Northern Command Depot at Ripon was one of the largest temporary camps in the country. Designed to house a transient population of over 30,000 troops, it had 26 miles of roads, 48 miles of sewers, a railway, and hundreds of huts, arranged in 44 large clusters. It was another city, bigger and busier than the old one it half-encircled.[1] If Owen arrived by the military railway, his first impression would have been of Army activity on a scale he had not seen in England since 1916: straight lines of huts, parade grounds, the rattle of musketry from the ranges, instructors shouting orders, thousands of men in training. He was allocated to a hut with thirteen other officers,

> 13 too many. Most of them are privates & sergeants in masquerade (as were half the officers at Clarence Gdns.) I'd prefer to be among honest privates than these snobs.

If the immediate future looked wretched, the longer prospect was worse. He told his mother he might be demobilized, but he can hardly have believed it.

Not everything was depressing. The hut was on Hellwath Common, an open plateau south-west of the town with a fine view of the cathedral towers. He made for them as soon as time allowed. Going in at the west door, he met a former Craiglockhart patient, J.C. Isaacson, who really had been demobilized as unfit. Isaacson had been a professional actor in the Benson theatre company before joining up and was now one again; there was to be a performance of *The Merry Wives* in the Garrison Theatre that evening. Owen had enjoyed the company's productions in the past and now had the chance to be introduced to Benson himself. He had tea with Isaacson and returned 'much bucked' to the camp.

He seems to have gone to the play and met the company, but the

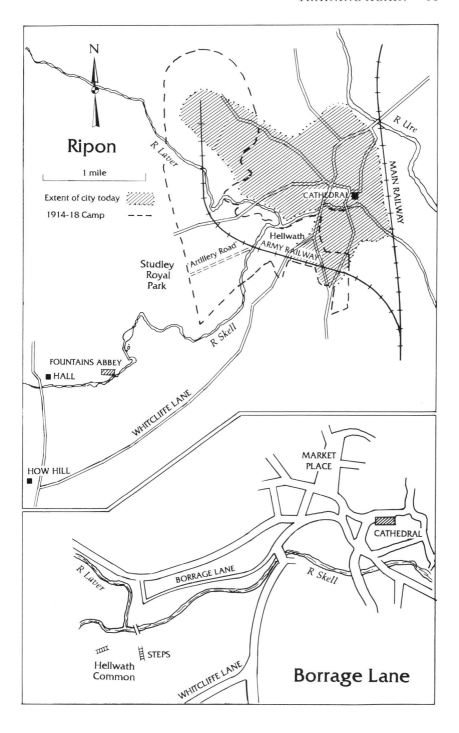

N

Ripon

1 mile

Extent of city today

1914-18 Camp

R Laver

R Ure

MAIN RAILWAY

CATHEDRAL

Hellwath

Artillery Road

ARMY RAILWAY

Studley
Royal
Park

R Skell

FOUNTAINS ABBEY
■ HALL

WHITCLIFFE LANE

HOW HILL
■

MARKET
PLACE

CATHEDRAL

R Laver

BORRAGE LANE

R Skell

Hellwath
Common

STEPS

WHITCLIFFE LANE

Borrage Lane

Hellwath Common and Ripon Cathedral. Owen's hut was probably somewhere on the left.

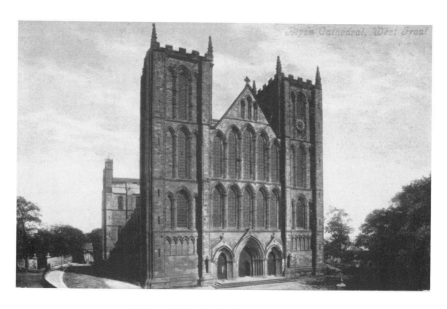

Ripon Cathedral: the west front.

Army tents on Hellwath, probably a Territorial camp before the war.

Left: Ripon huts in decay, probably some years after the war. Wartime pictures of the camp are apparently rare; photography of military subjects was strongly discouraged, except for propaganda purposes.

Right: A hut under construction at Ripon.

chance of a second meeting next day was lost when he was struck down with sudden fever. At the time he thought the cause was his 'extreme disgust' at the camp. Later he wondered whether he had not been a victim of the influenza that was beginning to sweep Europe. He had a 'perfectly ghastly night' in an isolation hut, sweating in muddy Army blankets and bloodstained sheets. If it was 'flu, he escaped lightly from an epidemic which was to kill more people than the war itself. He wrote home fairly cheerfully on 16 March and was discharged next day.

As the 17th was a Sunday, he had the whole day to himself and set off on a long walk into the country westwards, apparently not knowing that ahead of him was one of the most spectacular artificial landscapes in England. The camp lay between Ripon and the great estate of Studley Royal, which was open to any member of the public who signed the

Left: This track west of Ripon was 'Artillery Road' in the South Camp in 1915–18. Owen may have followed it to reach the gates of Studley Royal on 17 March.

Hercules and Antaeus, Studley Royal park.

book at the lodge and paid a shilling. He would have followed the great lime avenue through the deer park, turning down to the water gardens, where the little River Skell became a series of formal lakes, linked by canals and cascades. Among the temples and statuary subtly positioned along the wooded valley by eighteenth-century taste, he would have been amused to notice his old acquaintances, Hercules and Antaeus, wrestling in stone. A sharp turn in the path revealed the grandest sight of all, found quite by chance on a spring day: the ruins of Fountains Abbey.

As Blanche Bulman had found when she took him to Flodden in 1912, once he was interested in something he could keep going for hours. Beyond the abbey he came upon Fountains Hall, 'a glorious house. . . Almost worth fighting for!'. Further on he

noticed a kind of Watchtower or chapel on the top of a hill. It arrested

Fountains Abbey.

attention as all such towers do, and I climbed up, and finding inhabitants in it, desired tea of them. Only half the old chapel is occupied by peasants; the other is vacant. The rent would be about 2s. a week! The windows have a marvellous view (for this part of the world) & I could spend my spring evenings very pleasantly up there.

'A Tower far off arrests a man's eye always', he had written in his Outlook Tower essay. The building on How Hill seemed a possible successor to his Shrewsbury attic and the Scarborough turret. However, modern explorers of the hill have found 1914–18 buttons and cap badges, so it may have been a less isolated spot than a poet would have liked. It was much too far from the camp, in any case, as he probably realized during the long walk back.

On 18 March, his twenty-fifth birthday, he spent a quiet afternoon in the cathedral. If the comforts of Scarborough had begun to blunt his purpose, life at Ripon renewed his belief that he had a 'duty to perform towards War'. A present of chocolate from his sister reminded him of similar parcels received at the front; the tin had been crushed, and the

Fountains Hall.

How Hill tower, an eighteenth-century folly on the site of a medieval chapel. The two small cottages attached to the tower were occupied by farm labourers until the 1940s.

paper was spattered with blood, like the sheets in the camp hospital. He had to find somewhere to write. He set about getting fit, giving up alcohol and tobacco and starting each morning with a hot and cold shower at seven. 'From nine to about 3 p.m. we do physical, short walks, & Lectures. We are thus free all evening.' Work at Scarborough had sometimes continued into the night. The free time at Ripon could easily have been wasted: on the 19th he took a trip to Harrogate, which turned out to be dull, and the next day he walked a couple of miles to see

The cottage in Borrage Lane, Ripon, where Owen worked under the skylight.

some friends of the Gunstons, who turned out to be duller still. Two or three days later he discovered what he needed: 'a Room in a Cottage close to camp: the very thing'.

The spring offensive

On the northern edge of the common near the hut, a flight of steps led down to a footbridge across the Skell. A lane followed the stream towards the 'village-city', past paddocks, a few old houses, and an incongruous terrace of tiny cottages set back from the road, one of which had a room to let.

He found this haven within a day or two of 21 March, one of the most terrible dates in the history of the war. Shortly before dawn on that day, the Germans launched their long-expected onslaught on the Western Front, advancing fast, and in enormous strength, on a front of over forty miles. The main thrust was from St Quentin. On the hills above the

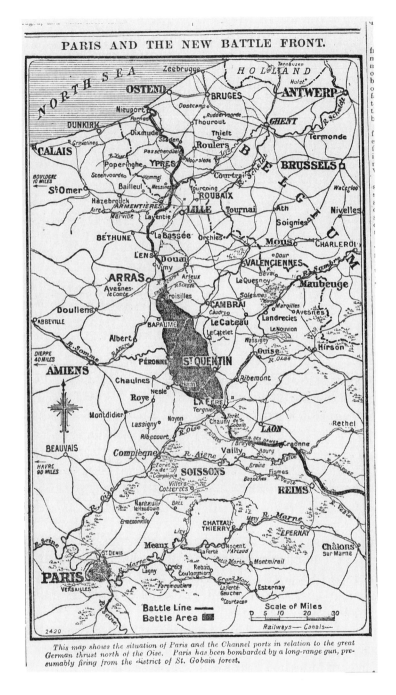

Map of the German advance, *The Times*, 25 March 1918.

town, only a field or two away from Savy Wood, men of the 16th Battalion, Manchester Regiment, peered through the morning fog as huge masses of men and armaments poured past, racing towards the old Somme battlefields. The Manchesters strengthened the quarry they were holding (it was the same one that Owen's battalion had captured a year before, and it was about to become famous as 'Manchester Hill'), and sent their last message: 'Goodbye'.

News of the disaster began to filter through next day, although it was a while before the public could see that a massive retreat was in progress. During the next few weeks the daily map in *The Times* showed a black bulge moving relentlessly westwards. Village names familiar and dreadful from 1916–17 came back into the news, as land gained in months of weary fighting was now lost in days. Owen knew the places all too well.

It is specially cruel for me to hear of all *we* gained by St. Quentin having been lost. They are dying again at Beaumont Hamel, which already in 1916 was cobbled with skulls.

In his mind's eye he could see 'the lands about St Quentin crawling with wounded'. The fighting in front of St Quentin hardly lasted a day; little more than a week after the attack began, the Germans crossed the Somme Canal at Cerisy, where Owen had hitched rides on the hospital barges in the previous spring. Amiens itself, the main British base in France, came within artillery range and looked likely to fall. Even Paris was not safe: shells began falling on the city from a huge gun somewhere in the St Gobain forest 75 miles away. A church was reported to have been hit during the Good Friday service on 29 March, with 75 people killed and 90 injured.

The Mystery Gun of St. Gobain Wood is about as romantic an episode as the whole war has provided. Paris, after all, has so many ugly buildings and unnecessary civilians . . . 160 casualties in a second or two, and that in the heart of the enemy country, is pretty work.

British casualty figures were not revealed. The daily rate of losses was higher in those few weeks than in any other battle of the war.

Any hopes Owen had entertained about peace negotiations or his own demobilization vanished immediately. 'I must buck up and get fit!'

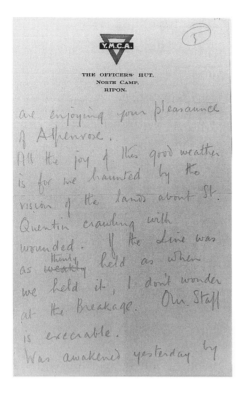

Part of an undated letter to Gunston. The first four pages are missing.
Alpenrose was the Gunstons' house, near Reading.

he told Gunston, in a letter that may have contained comments about
the Gunston family's safe life at home.[2] He wrote to his mother on Easter
Sunday:

> God so hated the world that He gave several millions of English-
> begotten sons, that whosoever believeth in them should not perish,
> but have a comfortable life.

News came from Scarborough that nearly all the boys in the barracks
and half the hundred officers now in the hotel were being sent out at
once.

A YMCA hut, Ripon, with its civilian staff.

Borrage Lane

In uncomfortable contrast to events in France, Ripon was turning out to be pleasanter than he had expected. If there was a spare hour, he could curl up in an armchair in the officers' YMCA hut, ignore the inevitable bridge players, and write letters home; sometimes there would even be a trio playing, 'making most lovely music'. Physical training was satisfying when he became good at it; the exercises for the mind which he had undergone at Craiglockhart were now complemented by exercises for the body, and his quick reactions seemed proof that he was 'completely restituted now from Shell Shock'. As soon as the day's exercises were over, he set off for his private world, noticing how the

'. . . by a happy little stream . . .': an old postcard of the River Skell near Borrage Lane, showing the steps up to Hellwath Common.

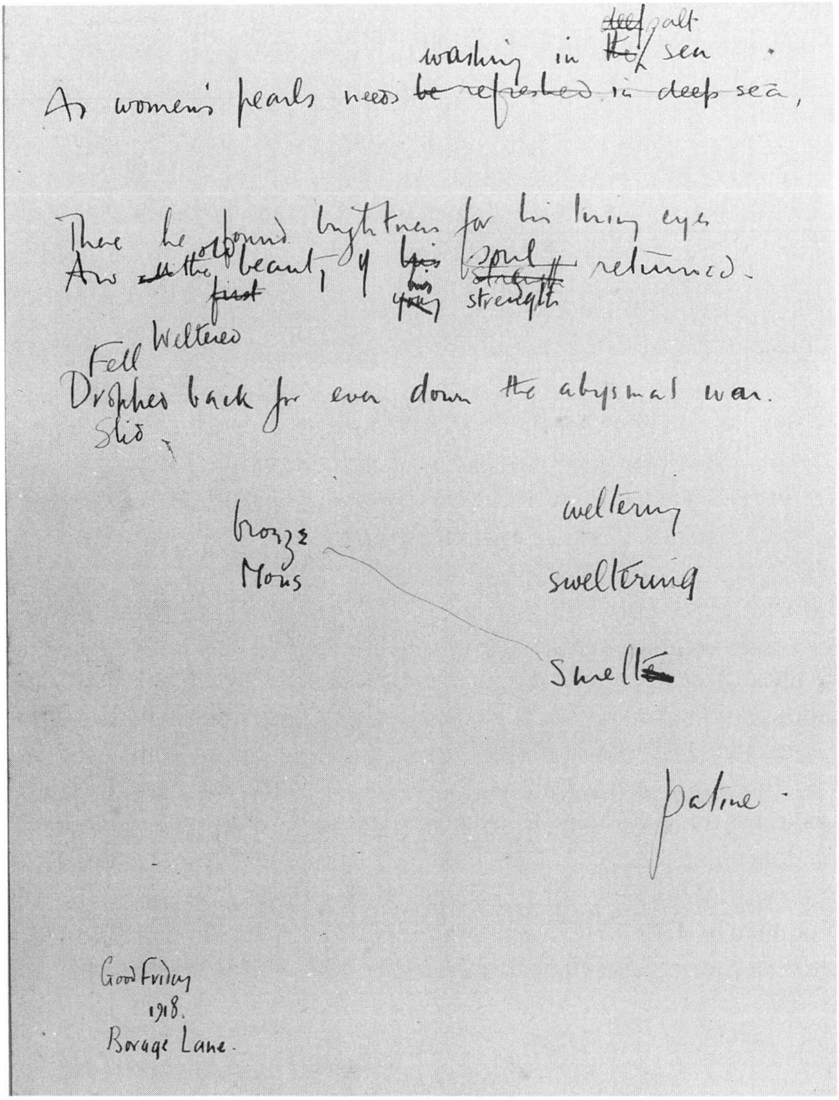

[handwritten manuscript draft]

washing in ~~the~~ ~~deep salt~~ sea .

As women's pearls need ~~be refreshed~~ in deep sea,

There he ~~found~~ brightness for his ~~loving~~ eyes
And ~~all the~~ ~~first~~ beauty of ~~his~~ ~~you~~ ~~soul~~ strength returned.

Fell / Weltered
~~Dropped~~ back for ever down the abysmal war.
Slid ,

bronze
Mons

weltering
sweltering
Smelt~~er~~

patine ·

Good Friday
1918.
Borrage Lane.

Rough work for the fragment, 'As bronze may be much beautified', dated Good Friday, Borrage Lane.

spring was advancing through the hedgerows and river banks. He had always thought of this season as the best time for writing poetry.

> The five minutes walk from Camp to my Cottage is by a happy little stream . . . / Ripon is only a mile from my hut, and through Borage Lane (my lane) it is an interesting walk; – especially this morning when the buds all made a special spurt between dawn and noon, and all the Lesser Celandines opened out together.[3]

Children in the lane played soldiers 'so piercingly' that he moved up into yet another attic, where there was only a skylight.

> It is a jolly Retreat. There I have tea and contemplate the inwardness of war, and behave in an owlish manner generally.
>   One poem have I written there; and thought another. I have also realised many defectuosities in older compositions.

He kept his retreat secret, presumably returning to the hut before lights out each evening.

Sitting under his skylight and contemplating the inwardness of war, Owen worked intensely. He had brought his old sonnets with him, a score of them neatly copied out and numbered, perhaps originally put together at the end of 1916 as a possible book like *The Nymph*. Most of them were exercises in the Decadent French style he had learned from Tailhade and others. He had been looking them over in Scarborough, but now, at last, they seemed irrelevant, mere 'Poetry'. He turned the pile over and used the reverse sides for new work. The first poem he 'thought' in the cottage may have been the unfinished fragment, 'As bronze may be much beautified', which he started on the back of an old sonnet on Good Friday. The first completed poem was perhaps 'Greater Love', also drafted on the backs of old sonnets. With their themes of sacrificial death, redemption, burial, and resurrection or the lack of it, these two pieces would have been relevant to that Easter, when God seemed to hate the world.[4]

'Insensibility', perhaps another Ripon poem, seems to show that he adopted Wordsworth's method of composing poetry from 'emotion recollected in tranquillity'. Wordsworth had daffodils to remember (Priestley sent some over from Scarborough at Easter), but Owen's memories were of grimmer subjects; the necessary mental state was

The Draft. Send-off.

Down the ~~deep~~ *close* darkening lanes they sang their way to the siding-shed.
To the siding-shed,
And ~~packed~~ *lined* the train with faces grimly gay.

Their breasts were stuck all white with wreath and spray
As men's are, dead.

Dull porters watched them, and a casual tramp
Stood staring hard,
Sorry to miss them from the upland camp.
Then signals, unmoved, signals
~~Unmoved, the signal~~ nodded, and a lamp
Winked to the guard.

So secretly, like wrongs hushed-up, they went.
They were not ours:
We never heard to which front these were sent.

Nor there if they yet mock what women meant
Who gave them flowers.

Shall they return to beatings of great bells
In wild trainloads?
A few, a few, too few for drums and yells,
May creep back, silent, to still village wells,
Up half-known roads.

The final draft of 'The Send-Off'.

'insensibility', rather than 'tranquillity'. Facing the 'phantoms of the mind' had brought on war dreams earlier in the year and might do so again. He put himself through the ordeal without help, alone, day after day, protecting himself with the nervelessness of the battle-hardened soldier:

> We wise, who with a thought besmirch
> Blood over all our soul,
> How should we see our task
> But through his blunt and lashless eyes?

His courage held. Sassoonish poems of 1917 were revised and in some cases rewritten. Poems drafted during the winter were completed; other winter work was incorporated into what became 'Exposure' and 'Strange Meeting'. New poems went from preliminary notes to final drafts. In little more than two months, most of his war poems were ready to show to Ross.

Several Borrage Lane poems seem appropriate to the locality. 'Arms and the Boy' was perhaps inspired by the children playing soldiers near the cottage. 'The Send-Off' describes a draft of men being marched away to entrain for France, a common sight around the camp after the March crisis. Details suggest the Ripon setting: white spring flowers; the 'close darkening lanes', warm even at dusk that year; the 'upland camp' on Hellwath Common; and the 'siding-shed' (one draft has 'rail-head') on the army railway. Owen's observations of 'the kind old sun' bringing seeds to life along the lane may have prompted 'Futility'. Just a year earlier he had spent several days and nights under shellfire above St Quentin; there had been snow as well as sunlight then, and 'Futility' is probably a memory of one of those bitter mornings.

'Strange Meeting', his most famous poem, seems likely to have been written in the cottage soon after the German offensive. It combines a Romantic vision with a shell-shock nightmare: the poet enters death's cave, which is also a dug-out, and meets an enemy he has killed. He discovers that the other man has held poetic hopes identical to his own. As Bertrand Russell had prophesied, the spiritual leaders of the future are slaughtering each other and there will be no true peace. As Owen contemplated his own predicament, he saw that the necessity of following Sassoon's example as an officer meant that he could not look forward to a larger destiny as a poet. He built into 'Strange Meeting' a revised version of 'Earth's wheels run oiled with blood', the lines he had addressed to his friend in the previous winter, altering the wording from hope to despair.

Strange Meeting.   3

It seemed that ~~from my dug out~~ out of the battle I escaped
Down some profounder tunnel, ~~older~~ dull long since scooped
Through granites which ~~the nether~~ ~~titanic~~ flames had groined.
                                    wars

~~Down all its length~~
Yet also there / encumbered sleepers groaned,
Too fast in thought or death to be bestirred.
Then, as I probed them, one sprang up, and stared
With piteous recognition in fixed eyes,
Lifting ~~his~~ distressful hands, as if to bless.
And by his smile, I knew we stood in Hell.
~~And By his~~ smile / I knew that sullen hall. —

Yet slumber droned all down that sullen hall
                            palms   visions,
With a thousand ~~fears~~ that ~~creature's~~ face was
                                                   groined;
Yet no blood reached him there from the upper ground,
And no ~~shell~~ thumped, or down the flues made moan.
        gun
But all was sleep. And no voice called for men.
"Strange friend", I said, "Here is no cause to mourn."
"None", said that other, "Save the undone years,
The ~~hopelessness~~. Whatever hope is yours,
Was my life also; ~~comrade~~. ~~I hunt~~ran wild
After the wildest beauty in the world,
Which lies not calm in eyes, or braided hair;

The second of two surviving drafts of 'Strange Meeting'.

But mocks the steady running of the hour.
And if it grieves, grieves richlier than here.
For by my glee might many men have laughed,
And of my weeping something had been left,
Which must die now. I mean the truth untold,
The pity of war, the ~~one~~ pity thing war distilled.
Now men will go content with what we spoiled,
Or, discontent, boil bloody, and be spilled.
They will be swift with swiftness of the tigress.
None will break ranks, though nations trek from
                                        progress.

Courage was mine, and I had mystery,
Wisdom was mine, and I had mastery:
To miss the march of this retreating world
Into vain citadels that are not walled. ~~Twheds~~
Then, when much blood had clogged their chariot
I would go ~~up~~ ~~the lie~~ and wash them from sweet wells,
Even ~~the truth~~ sank too deep for taint.
I would have poured my spirit without stint
But not ~~by my blood into~~ the ~~cess~~ of war.
~~through~~ wounds; not on ~~mure~~
Foreheads of men have bled where no wounds
                                        were.
I am the ~~enely~~ ~~German whom~~ you killed, my friend.
I ~~was a German conscript~~, ~~and you~~
I knew you in this dark: for so you frowned
Yesterday through me as you jabbed and killed.
I parried; but my hands were loath and cold.
  Let us sleep ~~now~~ . . . .

Mahim, the Owens' house in Monkmoor Road, Shrewsbury.
The plaque over the door commemorates the poet.

A family farewell

Word came from home that Owen's brother, Harold, was likely to be
sent on a dangerous naval mission (actually the Zeebrugge raid, for
which he was not in the end selected). The family wanted to gather for
what might be – and was – a last meeting. Owen managed to get forty-
eight hours' emergency leave.

By the evening of 9 April everyone was present: Tom, melancholy
and quiet, weary of office routine and anxious for Harold, his favourite;
Susan, motherly and perhaps a little tearful, urging everyone to eat;

Tom Owen, c.1920.   Susan Owen in July 1918.

Mary, tiny and doll-like, listening to her brothers' stories and probably saying nothing about the hospital where she was doing her bit for the war; Colin, hungry after farmwork and excited at the prospect of joining the RAF, now that his eighteenth birthday was approaching; Harold in sub-lieutenant's uniform; and Wilfred in khaki. They were there because Harold might soon be killed. When the meal was over, the two eldest brothers were tactfully left alone together. According to Harold's account, written long afterwards, they sat up all night, speaking only at rare intervals.[5]

Harold Owen could never forget that the few advantages their parents had been able to provide had been lavished on the eldest son. His own education was inadequate and unhappy. Throughout his later life he had to struggle with the burden of being a famous poet's brother. He tried to be an artist, then burned his paintings. As researchers began to ask questions, his judgement was overwhelmed by the family instinct for respectability. He clung to the manuscripts still in his possession (fortunately Sassoon had already steered many into the British Museum), anxiously filing, sorting, and, undoubtedly, censoring.[6] Much of this defensiveness sprang from an obsessive fear that the poet might be seen as homosexual. Harold's original motive in setting about

FOUND IN FATHER'S POCKET BOOK

Harold Owen in 1918. The
annotation is in his handwriting.

writing his memoirs was to portray the Wilfred he wanted the world to
believe in.

Most of the chapter in *Journey from Obscurity* about the gathering in
April 1918 is taken up by the two brothers' conversation. Wilfred
declares his determination to return to France: 'I know I shall be killed.
But it's the only place that I can make my protest from.' This is the
mythical Wilfred Owen speaking (the real one was elated a month later
when a home posting seemed likely). The talk moves on gingerly to
homosexuality, allowing for a strongly-worded denial by the author
that Wilfred was attracted to men. The manipulated dialogue is no
doubt based on a genuine memory, but what it reveals – unintentionally – is mutual incomprehension. The elder brother had much to
tell about Sassoon, Ross, and others, but Harold's evident revulsion at
the whole subject seemed to make confidences impossible.

Owen went up to his room at daybreak, not wanting to meet his
father over breakfast. It was a cold, wet morning, heavy cloud hiding
the Wrekin; he seems to have spent it asleep or browsing among his
books. He was still pulling books off the shelves when Harold went up to
fetch him in the afternoon. They walked to the station. Tom was
working elsewhere that day, but he had left instructions that his son
should be ushered into an empty compartment and the door locked to

keep other passengers out. Harold remembered his brother's parting words as being about the need to get money, the old family concern.

Later in the month Owen wrote to Gunston, who had left YMCA work and started a long career as an architect. Owen asked whether the new job would provide continuing exemption from military service, and added in a further dig at his cousin's conscience that he had himself been moved up 'to the 4th (of 6 Divisions) of Fitness. There is no doubt – from the elaborate soundings to which I'm subjected – that my heart is shock-affected.' Then he thought of Harold, who might at that moment be in danger: 'Harold has had some terrific adventures: but chiefly on land: & not connected with the war.' The younger brother had evidently been less reticent than his memoirs suggest. Although Gunston had a sense of humour and could be entrusted with secrets, Harold was more to be admired and even, perhaps, to be envied.

London

By May Owen had enough new poems to warrant a trip to Half Moon Street. His mother wanted him to visit her again and kept writing plaintively about the state of her health. Reading one of her letters during the 'stand-easies' of physical drill, he felt some impatience. She ought to do exercises too, he told her, and perhaps try visiting the local orphanage. On Thursday 16 May he set off for London. Nellie Burton was able to provide a whole flat above Ross's this time; Owen had the use of it for three nights, 'for 7/6 with breakfast! And I had more invitations to lunch & dinner than I could manage!'

After lunch with Ross at the Reform on the Friday, he spent the afternoon at the War Office in Whitehall with Scott Moncrieff, who had been working there since March. Scott Moncrieff's job enabled him to recommend instructors for cadet battalions; he had already found Graves an enjoyable posting in Wales. Offering to put Owen's name forward for an instructorship, he introduced him to friendly colleagues and convinced him that there was every chance of success. Owen seems to have been more than willing to be nominated; his letters during the next few weeks show no sign of any revival of his New Year feeling that he ought to 'go back' to be with the troops. He had done his bit at the

Projects . (May 5 · 1918 . Ripon)

1. To write blank-verse plays on old Welsh themes . Models: Tennyson , Yeats , 1920 .

2. Collected Poems . (1919)

3. Perseus .

4. Idyls in Prose .

Owen had no intention of remaining exclusively a 'war poet', but until he met the Sitwells, heralds of Modernism, his plans were old-fashioned.

front, Scott Moncrieff would have told him. If Graves could accept a home posting, so should he. He might first be sent on a course at the School of Instruction at Berkhamsted, as Graves had been earlier in the month.[7]

The response to Owen's new poems in the golden room was 'magnificent', and the talk seemed to go on all night. More Adey was so impressed with a draft of 'Mental Cases' that he insisted it should not be sent to *The English Review* because the *Review* '"should not be encouraged".!!!!'. A plot was laid that Owen should have his work typed and sent to Heinemann, who would be sure to ask Ross for an opinion. 'Ross first meant to take it himself but we thought this independent idea a great joke.' Ross ''phoned round' another young disciple of Sassoon's, Osbert Sitwell, warning him not to frighten the new poet, who was certain to be nervous at meeting a real baronet's son.

In the end it was Sitwell, more than six months later, who made the first moves towards getting a book published. Despite all the excitement, Owen's plans never even reached the typing stage. Time ran out on him. It ran out on Ross, too. Pemberton Billing's vilification of *Salome*

THE SONG OF ROLAND

To MR W. O.

To you, my master in assonance, I dedicate my part in this assonant poem: that you may cover the faults in my handiwork with the protection of your name. Poor English I have written, yet have translated faithfully — in hundreds of lines have reproduced almost identically ~~the~~ Turold's own language. And my sole merit — other than your patronage — may be this that I send my readers back to the old Chanson which has been, in England, too easily forgotten. at this time lessons are to be found in the Song of Roland that ~~we may~~ all of us may profitably learn — To pursue chivalry, to avoid treachery ~~and punish~~, to rely upon our own resources, ~~and~~ and to fight uncomplaining when support is withheld from us ; to live, in fine, honourably and to die gallantly. So I have worked and written that the song our Saxon forebears heard our Norman forbears shout at Hastings — may not be altogether unheard in their children's armies.

C. K. SCOTT MONCRIEFF

Scott Moncrieff's original dedication to his translation of the *Song of Roland*, the medieval French epic. He gave this manuscript to Owen in the summer of 1918. The translation as published in 1919 has a different dedication: a Shakespearian sonnet to Owen, and poems to Bainbrigge and another friend.

had provoked the leading actress into suing for libel, and the case opened ten days after Owen's London visit, soon developing into a display of public hysteria. Lord Alfred Douglas attacked Ross from the witness box. Ross's frail health showed signs of giving way, to the distress of his friends, and Owen would not have felt able to ask him for any further help.

The May weekend in London continued to be eventful. Scott Moncrieff was in love, and he was not the sort of man to be satisfied with words. By the Sunday things had gone too far for Owen. A literary parallel suggested itself to Scott Moncrieff's curious imagination. Just as 'Mr W.H.' had eluded Shakespeare, yet been the 'onlie begetter' of the sonnets, so 'Mr W.O.' had refused proffered love, yet been an inspiration for the rhymes which Scott Moncrieff was using in translating the *Song of Roland*. It seemed worth exploring both relationships in a series of Shakespearian sonnets, and Scott Moncrieff wrote out a sonnet then and there on Half Moon Street paper (Owen added the date).

> Remembering rather all my waste of days
>   Ere I had learned the wonders thou hast shewn
> Blame not my tongue that did not speak thy praise
>   Having no language equal to thine own
> Blame not my eyes that, from their high aim lowered
>   Yet saw there more than other eyes may see:
> Nor blame head heart hands feet that, overpowered
>   Fell at thy feet to draw thy heart to me.
> Blame not me all that all was found unworthy
>   But let me guard some fragment of thy merit,
> That, though myself in th' earth dissolve, being earthy,
>   In thy long fame some part I may inherit.
> So through the ages, while the bright stars dwindle
>   At thy fresh sun my moon's cold face I'll kindle.
>
>   May 19, 1918

More sonnets followed. In his only surviving letter to Owen, dated 26 May from the War Office, their author explained what he was trying to do:

> No sealing up of the fount of passion is indicated by the cessation of the flow of sonnets – but simply an inflow of work here . . . you

mustn't take them too seriously. It's vivisection really – of both you and me. I want very much to be able to add to the Shakespeare controversy a conclusive word based on experience. I feel pretty certain that Shakespeare selected some wight to whom he sent 'From fairest creatures' [the first of the Sonnets] in a letter. He then went on with them – bringing in a few passing events and current relations . . .[8]

Scott Moncrieff added: 'Hurry up and send me *Aliens* ['Mental Cases']. Either *Aliens* or *Aliens of War* you must call it. Alter that line about experience – and I'll try to get it into the [F]ortnightly.' He was helpful on matters of wording and publication, as Graves had found during the winter, and in return Owen took an interest in the *Song of Roland*. 'Any success I may have had', Scott Moncrieff wrote of the translation in 1919, '. . . was due entirely to Owen's example, criticism and encouragement.' When he sent Owen the first pages in the summer of 1918, they were prefaced by a dedication 'To Mr W.O.'

Two other extant sonnets hint at 'shame' and 'scandal'. That could refer either to Owen's Army record, for Scott Moncrieff had access to confidential files, or to gossip among Ross's friends. Graves said many years afterwards that he heard about Scott Moncrieff's behaviour from Ross; he was often unreliable, but his lively correspondence with Scott Moncrieff does seem to have stopped abruptly in May 1918 and his later comments about Owen show little of the enthusiasm he had expressed in the previous winter. Scott Moncrieff remained on close terms with Owen, but the brief reminiscences he published in 1920–21 betray jealousy and resentment towards the dead poet's friends, who in turn ignored his contribution to Owen's achievement. He felt he knew Owen better than Sassoon did. Sassoon thought he was thoroughly objectionable.

Sassoon returned to France in May 1918. He had been sent to Ireland and then Palestine, before being brought back with thousands of others to strengthen the line after the March crisis. While he was on the boat he composed an epilogue to his poems of protest; they seemed useless now.

> For the last time I say – War is not glorious,
> Though lads march out superb and fall victorious, –
> Scrapping like demons, suffering like slaves,

Owen walked from Ripon to Aldborough on a fine spring day in 1918. These two shelters in what was then the pub garden protect mosaics, relics of the large Roman town of Isurium. Before the war he had often dug at Uriconium, a similar site near Shrewsbury.

And crowned by peace, the sunlight on their graves.

You swear we crush The Beast: I say we fight
Because men lost their landmarks in the night,
And met in gloom to grapple, stab, and kill,
Yelling the fetish-names of Good and Ill
That have been shamed in history.

O my heart,

Be still; you have cried your cry; you have played your part.

('Testament')[9]

Sassoon sent a copy of this to Owen, who learned it by heart. It seemed more convincing than the chivalric affirmations in Scott Moncrieff's flattering dedication to the *Song of Roland*. And if there was any truth in the parallel drawn in that dedication between medieval brothers-in-arms and modern soldiers, it hardly reinforced the idea that a fit man could honourably apply for a home posting.

'My subject is War'

It was probably in the three weeks after his London visit that Owen roughed out a preface and scheme of contents for a book. Friends and family were keen to see him in print, but he refused to hurry, determined to learn from Gunston's rashness. 'I can now write so much better than a year ago', he told Mary on 29 May, 'that for every poem I add to my list I subtract one from the beginning of it. You see I take myself solemnly now, and that is why, let me tell you, once for all, I refrain from indecent haste in publishing.' The book would be a collection of about thirty war poems, arranged with a strong didactic purpose. Many of the thousands of poetry books published during the war were didactic and many had prefaces. Almost invariably they aimed to extol the nation or the troops, or to console the bereaved. Owen's book would be different; his Preface explicitly disavows the usual aims. 'This book is not about heroes . . . Nor is it about deeds or lands . . . These elegies are to this generation in no sense consolatory . . . All a poet can do today is warn [children].'

The Preface, surviving only as one scrawled fragment, has become one of the most famous documents in modern literature. Twentieth-century poets have tended to confine themselves to small topics, shunning didacticism and preoccupying themselves with language and technique. Yeats said in 1916 that all a poet could do during the war was to keep silent.[10] Owen felt no such limitations. He devoted himself with evangelizing zeal to one immense subject, in complete confidence that a poet could and should tackle it and that poetry was the human spirit's strongest defence against hate and aggression. In this he took his stand with the Romantics; he was perhaps the last great heir of Wordsworth and Shelley, both of whom had made comparable claims for poetry a century or so earlier. He rejected most wartime verse, either because it was 'Poetry' of the kind he, Gunston, and many others had been content with for so long, or because it concealed the truth of war under a mist of consolatory rhetoric. Like the Modernists – of whom he knew nothing in May 1918 – he was an innovator in words and technique; unlike them, he wrote directly about the war with the authority of experience.

'My subject is War, and the pity of War.' The list of contents which accompanies the Preface suggests what he meant. Each poem is given a 'Motive'. The poems in the first half of the book are grouped under

Owen's Preface, probably drafted at Borrage Lane in late May or early June 1918.

'Protest'. Then the theme changes through 'Cheerfulness', 'Description', and 'Grief', to 'Philosophy'. The most shocking poems are in the first half. Pity had to be based on knowledge, a knowledge stripped of the

The list of contents accompanying the Preface.

usual heroic rhetoric. Only after that could the reader be allowed to move on to grief and reflection. 'These elegies' were not to be elegiac in any merely sorrowful sense, yet Sassoonish protest was not enough; the final stage was 'pity'.

Another list, probably drawn up at Borrage Lane in May.

The two surviving versions of Owen's 'list' suggest that few, if any, of his war poems have been lost, whatever else his brother may have destroyed. With one or two exceptions, all the titles can be attached to known poems.[11] One of the lists is headed with the proposed title of the book: 'Disabled and Other Poems'. Overleaf he made a note of people who ought to be sent copies: Sassoon, Graves, the Poetry Bookshop, his principal sources of advice; Mrs Gray, Dr Brock, Mrs Fullerton, Miss Wyer, the Astronomer Royal, in Edinburgh; Bainbrigge, Meiklejohn, and a few others. (Ross and Scott Moncrieff are not mentioned, probably because he took them for granted, having just seen them.)

His time at Ripon was almost over. The camp which had seemed 'awful' in March had become 'the pleasantest . . . I know' by May. He went river-bathing in the hot sunshine and sent home for a tennis racket. By 21 May he had been promoted to the second division of fitness. A few days later he met a drummer called George, whom he had known at Dunsden before the war. Drummers were boys too young to fight: George must have been about eleven or twelve in the days when Owen was taking choir practices and Sunday School outings. The parish children had been the lay assistant's chief comfort; meeting one of them now was an emotional experience, which is no doubt why Owen's account of it is now 'missing'. He seems to have talked to the boy for hours, reviving old memories.

On 4 June he was called before a Medical Board and graded fit for General Service. 'Drummer George of Dunsden *wept* when I said goodbye. (I had seen him 3 times!) This you must not tell *anybody*. Such things are not for this generation of vipers.' There was an evening for packing up and clearing the cottage room. Next afternoon he was back in Scarborough. His father sent a message: 'gratified to know you are normal again'.

— 5 —

GENERAL SERVICE

No call from the War Office

ON 5 June Owen reported to the barracks outside Scarborough, as he had done seven months earlier. This time there was no move to the comforts of Clarence Gardens. The battalion had apparently vacated the hotel, now that so many officers had been sent out to France. Fortunately Priestley was still mess president. He had kept in touch and was still negotiating for a chest of drawers which Owen had spotted during one of their tours of the antique shops. Kind-hearted 'Uncle Henry' knew that his young protégé was likely to be depressed by the harsh life ahead. He welcomed him with 'a private tea – fine China tea, – in priceless porcelain'. The mess president was entitled to a set of three rooms in one of the old barrack buildings. Owen had no such privilege:

I live in a tent with a cinder floor, a yard or two from the Main Entrance to Camp; so it is inundated with vile dust. Thus it is not necessary to try to grit my teeth: it is done without effort.

We get up at six, and work furiously till 6 p.m., after which we are too tired to move.

Priestley is powerless to give me a room in Barracks as all A officers must sleep under canvas.

I have informed the War Office of my Category & address. I cannot keep alive here long. Here one does not live at all. One eats, (badly) sleeps, (well) and works like a demented piece of clockwork.[1]

The next month or two became a period of cruel uncertainty. A reply soon came from the War Office that he might be sent on a month's course at Berkhamsted and then as an instructor to cadets in his old regiment, the Artists' Rifles. No confirmation followed. 'Nothing to report from War Office', he wrote on 21 June. Three days later, when the Monday mail brought no news, he seems to have realized that the

126

The former Northern Cavalry Barracks at Burniston, Scarborough.

The parade ground, Scarborough barracks.

Owen's silver cigarette case,
with his monogram.

chance had gone. 'As no call has come from the W.O. . . . I shall likely be
here another month – unless drafted out, which is *not* probable.' The
last four words may have been added to reassure his mother.

Unless Owen's files one day emerge from the vast archives of the
Ministry of Defence, it will probably never be possible to reconstruct
exactly what happened.[2] Apparently the General Staff approved Scott
Moncrieff's nomination of him as an instructor, but the Adjutant-
General's Department rejected it, insisting that every able-bodied man
was wanted for the front. After 24 June all references to a home posting
vanish from Owen's letters. Perhaps it was no coincidence that his war
dreams began again, although to his mother he blamed the tent canvas
flapping all night in high winds or the 'hideous faces of the Advancing
Revolver Targets' he had been firing at. The irascible Colonel Mitchell,
who was still commanding the battalion, would not have responded
kindly to enquiries from London about an instructorship. Owen had
been sent to Ripon to get fit for active service, and now he had to be
retrained in the task he had failed in, leading men in the field. He could
learn that in Scarborough by instructing conscripts.

They certainly needed it, Owen thought, looking at the newcomers. Most of them were factory workers from Lancashire, just turned eighteen, 'awful specimens', pale, thin, and undernourished. Only a few Welshmen and 'Shropshire lads', whose accents he recognized with pleasure, seemed strong enough to cope. Yet somehow training would turn them all into 'mahogany swashbucklers' like the fit men who were ready to be sent out. He worked hard in this deadly Boys' Training Club, teaching them the routines of soldiering: musketry, map-reading, standing still on parade, keeping their feet clean. The more competent they could become at these things, the greater their chances of survival. He could be of use to them and he knew it. He worked for their sakes and to keep his mind steady, and the more they came to rely on him the more he understood that he ought to be with them, not with officer-cadets.

Wheels

As usual, his gloom at being in a new place lifted after a while. Priestley managed to get him a single tent, the only one available. It was waterproof and surrounded by long grass and buttercups, so there was less damp and dust to contend with. When he had time, which was seldom, he could retreat to Priestley's rooms, where his host would sometimes provide tea and even strawberries.

Having at first expected not to be in Scarborough long, he had 'magnificently resolved' not to unpack books and papers, but on 15 June:

> lo! an urgent request from the Sitwells in London for more of my poems for their 1918 Anthology which is coming out immediately. This is on the strength of 'The Deranged' ['Mental Cases'], which S. Moncrieff showed them the other day. I know not what to do. For one thing I want to see the Sitwells' etc. works before I decide to co-appear in a book!

On that same day 'Futility' and 'Hospital Barge' were published in *The Nation*. Letters came from Sassoon, and later a copy of his new book, *Counter-Attack*, containing poems he had read to Owen at Craiglock-

Poetry.

HOSPITAL BARGE.

BUDGING the sluggard ripples of the Somme
A barge round old Cèrisy slowly slewed.
Softly her engines down the current screwed,
And chuckled softly with contented hum,
Till fairy tinklings struck their crooning dumb.
The waters rumpling at the stern subdued :
The lock-gate took her bulging amplitude :
Gently from out the gurgling lock she swum.

One reading by that calm bank shaded eyes
To watch her lessening westward quietly.
Then, as she neared the bend, her funnel screamed.
And that long lamentation made him wise
How unto Avilon in agony
Kings passed in the dark barge which Merlin dreamed.

FUTILITY.

Move him into the sun—
Gently its touch awoke him once,
At home, whispering of fields half-sown.
Always it woke him, even in France,
Until this morning and this snow.
If anything might rouse him now
The kind old sun will know.

Think how it wakes the seeds—
Woke once the clays of a cold star.
Are limbs, so dear-achieved, are sides
Full-nerved, still warm, too hard to stir?
Was it for this the clay grew tall?
—O what made fatuous sunbeams toil
To break earth's sleep at all?

WILFRED OWEN.

Two poems in *The Nation*, 15 June 1918, and a preliminary version of one of them.

hart. No doubt books and papers were unpacked after all, and Priestley's rooms became a haven a little like the Ripon cottage.

Owen 'broke out of camp' to order the anthology, *Wheels 1917*. The bookshops were reluctant to send for a publication they regarded as unsaleable, but he persisted so long that an assistant caused a sensation by exclaiming that he must be '"Osbert himself"'. (The Sitwells were known in Scarborough, where their father had a fine house in town.) Osbert sent him an epigram about the fierce old premier of France, Clemenceau, being 'fully satisfied' with the Crucifixion (newspapers often reported that Clemenceau was 'fully satisfied' with news from the front). Owen wrote back:

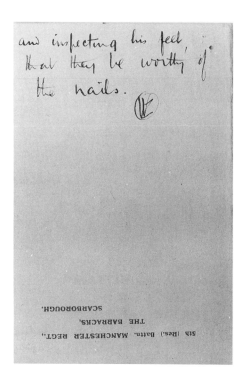

'Ill Winds.

Up on the cross in ugly agony
The Son of God hung dying; & the roar
Of earthquakes rent the solemn sky,
and tore

The dead from out their graves.
And Jesus died.

But M. Clemenceau was fully satisfied.

I need not show unto you this
Jesus. For myself, I have seen
him with my eyes, and touched
his blood with my hands.

I am now engaged in teaching
him to lift his cross by numbers,

and inspecting his feet,
that they be worthy of
the nails.

SCARBOROUGH,
THE BARRACKS,
5th (Res.) Battn. MANCHESTER REGT.,

Osbert Sitwell's epigram, copied out by Owen and sent home with a comment.
The pencil annotation is by Harold Owen.

I rehearsed your very fine epigram upon our Mess President – rather a friend of mine. He did not immediately recognise Jesus. The rest of the Mess would not of course know the name of Monsieur Clemenceau ... May I send 'Ill Winds' to a French youth who might translate and circulate it where it would be appreciated?

The letter to Sitwell is a rare example of Owen writing to someone he did not know well. Still a little in awe of his correspondent, he takes the chance to present himself as friendly with the mess president and with literary people in France (he was still in correspondence with at least one of his Bordeaux pupils). He writes as one Aesthete to another, and in that spirit, taking his cue from the epigram, he composes a famous paragraph, an elaborate conceit almost worthy of Wilde:

For 14 hours yesterday I was at work – teaching Christ to lift his cross

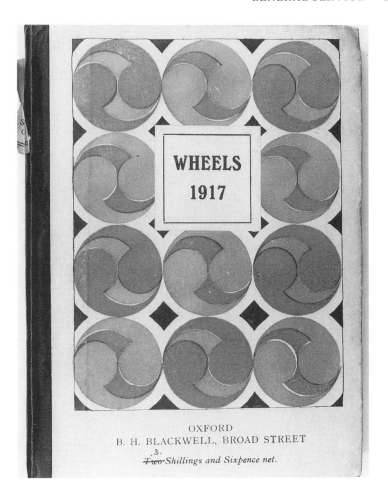

WHEELS
1917

OXFORD
B. H. BLACKWELL, BROAD STREET
.3.
~~Two~~ Shillings and Sixpence net.

Owen's copy of *Wheels 1917*.

by numbers, and how to adjust his crown; and not to imagine he thirst till after the last halt; I attended his Supper to see that there were no complaints; and inspected his feet to see that they be worthy of the nails. I see to it that he is dumb and stands to attention before his accusers. With a piece of silver I buy him every day, and with maps I make him familiar with the topography of Golgotha.

Owen read *Wheels* with interest. Edited by Edith Sitwell in typically controversial mood, it was the first anthology of British verse to be

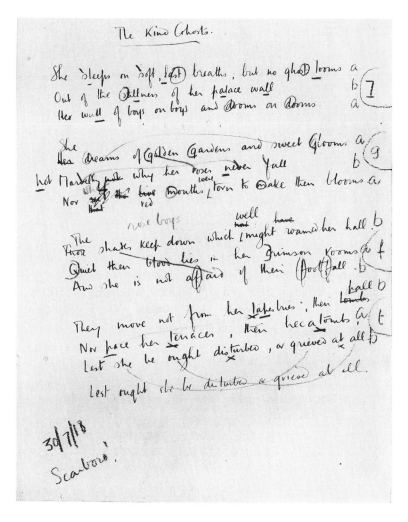

The only surviving manuscript of 'The Kind Ghosts'. Owen has marked in the rhymes.

deliberately avant-garde. Traditions of technique and subject were flouted. There was a curiously pervasive imagery of streets: 'the sad houses sleep', 'Gaunt figures haunt the narrow streets', 'pale tinged houses dream', 'Places to scribble our names on, seats, lamp-posts and walls', 'The weathercocks fly helter-skelter', 'Blind windows face the interminable road'. Whether or not this represented the sickness of civilian England, the book's political stance – very unlike that of other wartime anthologies – was certainly one that Owen could approve of: all the *Wheels* poets seemed to loathe the war.

Whenever he found a new sort of poetry, he looked at it carefully to see what he could learn. Some lines which he wrote at the barracks show him working with the new style.

> The roads also have their wistful rest
> When the weather-cocks perch still & roost . . .
> The old houses muse of the old days . . .
>   And the dead scribble on walls . . .
> Though their own child cry for them in tears
> Women weep but hear no sound . . .

That 'also' in the first line may imply a link with 'The Kind Ghosts', a strange poem about a woman resting in a palace built out of the corpses of young men. Owen may have been planning a series of poems on wartime Britain, the quiet world of old streets and summer gardens where people dreamed of the past and ignored the present.

He seems to have failed to send the Sitwells anything until he met Osbert again in August. During his last few days in Scarborough, at the end of that month, he said he was hurriedly assembling poems for *Wheels*; it was presumably then that he drew up a shortlist of about eight titles and sent Osbert the eight manuscripts which remain in the Sitwell family collection. The deadline for the 1918 volume had passed, but the Sitwells kept their word. Soon after Owen's death, his mother wrote to Osbert, who confirmed that a selection of poems would appear in *Wheels 1919* and recommended that a book should be published, with an introduction by Sassoon. Mrs Owen sent a large batch of manuscripts, probably the contents of the file which Owen had marked 'Completed War Poems'; from these, Edith Sitwell chose seven poems for the anthology, dedicating the volume to his memory. Thus Owen appeared among Modernists, rather than the Georgians with whom he had proudly associated himself in the winter of 1917–18, and it was *Wheels*, not *Georgian Poetry*, which first brought him to public attention. Edith then edited the principal war poems for a book, not very accurately, and Sassoon wrote the introduction; *Poems by Wilfred Owen* came out in 1920.[3]

Second Lieutenant

Owen was fitter than he had ever been. He proved to be more accurate with a revolver than most of his colleagues (at the front later he brought down a man at about thirty yards). When the boys started dropping on parade 'like flies' from influenza, he astonished everyone by remaining immune. On 26 June he went for a cross-country run ('Have seldom enjoyed any exercise so much') and wrote a little poem about it.

> My lips, panting, shall drink space, mile by mile;
> Strong meats be all my hunger; my renown
> Be the clean beauty of speed and pride of style.

Then he refereed a football match. It all seemed quite out of character for someone who had once been considered sickly. 'I have just been playing a little cricket with the lads', he said casually one Sunday evening, adding that walking in the town had become intolerably boring. One reason for this sudden enthusiasm for sport must have been that it was the only way of socializing with the 'lads'; Army convention allowed a degree of equality only on the games field. He felt rather pleased with his new self.

He was participating in something absurdly close to the public school life he had always wanted. Like house prefects, the officers had to busy themselves sharing out responsibilities, organizing games, maintaining privileges, and making sure that everyone was as keen as mustard. The Army even preserved the fagging system. Each officer had a personal servant, chosen from the ranks, who would look after his possessions, bring him shaving water in the morning, and act as his bodyguard when they reached the battlefield. When Owen was about to go into the line in January 1917, he chose a servant 'for his excellence in bayonet work'. On his return to Scarborough in June 1918, he selected 'a Herefordshire gardener's boy', preferring someone from his own Welsh border country to the Lancashire mill hands; presumably this was 'little Jones', who figures in later letters.

Owen's duties varied. When he was battalion orderly officer, work went on until midnight. There was a gas course for a week, with an exam for the whole of the Saturday morning. That Saturday afternoon he had to pay the coast patrols twelve miles away, fortunately getting a

The Officers' Mess, a former private
house, in the barracks at
Scarborough.

lift on a motorbike. 'They complain of Loneliness. My stars!' In mid-July
he was battalion messing officer for ten days, directly responsible to the
colonel for feeding a thousand men. It was a much larger, less refined
job than catering for eighty or so officers at the hotel. The cookhouse
stank in the hot weather. An order came through that boys under
nineteen should be given extra meat and bread, so he had to separate
them from the older men at mealtimes.

> I have never in my life had to appear so omniscient & omnipotent. Nor
> have I ever struggled so desperately or so vainly against dirt &
> disorder. I put on overalls & whitewashed the cookhouse myself this
> morning!

A 'little army of W.A.A.C.s' did the cooking and washing up.

> It is almost impossible to control them. They either weep or take flight
> when reprimanded. 2 of Priestley's deserted today. One of 'mine'
> 'cries' several times every day.
>   Their work it is true is terribly hard; but I was responsible for the
> men's food, and had to 'slave' them. Tell Mary I overheard one

W.A.A.C. say after me 'I'd like to smack 'is brown face forrim.'

No sooner had the usual messing officer returned from leave than Priestley had to go into hospital and asked Owen to take his place as mess president. Colonel Mitchell was away, but Priestley must have known that he would not have approved, especially as mess presidents were normally majors. Owen was still a second lieutenant; he had confidently expected to 'put up' another pip in the previous December, but seven months later he was still wearing only one 'because nobody knows whether I am Lieut. or not'. Mitchell must have had a hand in the delay.[4]

Before Priestley left, the deal for the chest of drawers was completed. Owen sent the chest by rail to Shrewsbury, filling it with other winter purchases which he had presumably been storing in Priestley's rooms. For a few days the temporary mess president enjoyed the luxury of living in the three-roomed apartment and cycling into town every morning to find good food for the officers. Then the colonel returned and sent him back to his tent. The new president, Major Fletcher, was pleasant, but no substitute for 'Uncle Henry'.

There was nothing for it but to continue camp routine and wait for further orders. At that juncture, in the last week of July, news came which changed everything: '*Siegfried is in London, the victim of a British Sniper.*'

'The Greatest friend'

Earlier in July Owen had known Sassoon was 'in the forefront of the battle' and had written to cheer him up. Actually Sassoon had been remarkably cheerful at times in France. Taking care of his men seemed a more honourable task than teaching cadets how to fight, as Graves was doing in Wales. Graves wrote to Sassoon in verse:

> Poor Fusilier aggrieved with fate . . .
> Now your brief letters home pretend
> Anger and scorn that this false friend
> This fickle Robert . . .

Sassoon in camp.

Preaches 'The Bayonet' to Cadets
On a Welsh hill-side, grins, forgets. . . .
'*Guilty*' I plead and by that token
Confess my haughty spirit broken
And my pride gone; now the least chance
Of backward thought begins a dance
Of marionettes that jerk cold fear
Against my sick mind: . . .
                                    . . . till again
I view that dread La Bassée plain . . .[5]

Owen probably felt a similar mixture of inner guilt and fear, with the difference that Graves had tried hard to return to the front. Graves never quite recovered from shell-shock; even in old age, he would disconcert his friends by suddenly diving for shelter, as though the guns were firing again.

While Graves was finishing his poem in the second week of July, Sassoon was not far from La Bassée. It was entirely his own decision to

The only known letter from Sassoon to Owen (the slightly earlier letter which Owen sent home has not survived). Sassoon confused the date: 8 August 1918 was a Thursday.

go on patrol in No Man's Land early on the 13th. Taking a corporal with him, he crawled for two hours or so towards a German machine gun post. Dawn was beginning by the time they got close, so they hurled their bombs and fled. Halfway back they reached a sunken road, well out of sight of the enemy. Delighted with his adventure, Sassoon took his helmet off, stood up, and was shot in the head. One of his own sergeants had mistaken him for a German.

At the base hospital the internal debate which had plagued him at Craiglockhart began again. He wanted to get back to his battalion.

Why should I be the only one? They'd only think me a fool, ...
And then in my heart I know that it is the only way I can keep my soul clean, and vindicate my pride in the men who love and trust me. It is the supreme thing that is asked of me. And already I am shying at it.

'We'll be sending you across to England in a few days,' murmurs the nurse who is washing my blood-clotted hair. And my heart stops beating for a moment.[6]

Three days later he arrived at the American Red Cross Hospital at Lancaster Gate, overlooking Hyde Park. A distraught poem he sent to Graves records that Marsh, Ross, Meiklejohn, Robert Nichols, and Osbert Sitwell 'arrived in crowd'. 'Jabber – Gesture – Jabber – Gesture – Nerves went phut and failed'. The only visitors allowed in after that were Rivers, his doctor from Craiglockhart, and Ross, the two men best able to calm him.

Owen was almost due for leave. He tried in vain to persuade his mother to come up to Scarborough, so that he would have time to visit London. A letter from Sassoon ended all uncertainty about what he had to do. He sent it home: '. . . a precious letter, from the Greatest friend I have . . . Now must I throw my little candle on his torch, and go out again. / There are rumours of a large draft of officers shortly.' The contents of Sassoon's letter can be guessed at from his diary entry. Unlike some of the jabberers, Owen understood. His 'Greatest friend' was Sassoon, not Scott Moncrieff, and the place for a true poet and fit officer was in the line. Presumably he applied to join the forthcoming draft.

There was another 'black week' in the camp. Heavy rain flooded the tent for two days. A ship had been torpedoed off Scarborough a month earlier and there seems to have been a local panic; the attack on the town in 1914 had not been forgotten. There were several practice alarms in the small hours, when the battalion was called out to man the coastal defences, and these early starts were not compensated for by reduced working hours. Owen spent long, wet days on the firing range. He said on 8 August that leave seemed impossible for at least another week, not knowing that the military machine had already begun to work.

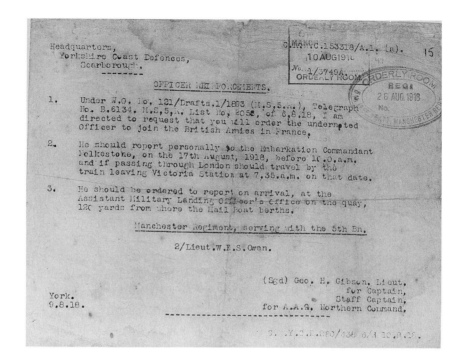

The first embarkation order, 9 August.

'And this time I must go'

On 9 August the Northern Command at York sent a message to the barracks. 'Under W.O. No. 121/Drafts. 1/1893 (M.S.5.R.), Telegraph No. B.6134. M.S.5.R. List No. 2058, of 6.8.18', the War Office had directed that Second Lieutenant W.E.S. Owen should be ordered to join the British Armies in France, embarking from Folkestone on the 17th. The message was received by the Orderly Room at Scarborough on the 10th, and Owen wrote home at once to say he had been told to attend a medical inspection next day (Sunday) with the twenty-one other officers who were expecting to be drafted.

It was a relief. 'I am glad. That is I am much gladder to be going out again than afraid. I shall be better able to cry my outcry, playing my part.'[7] The time had come for him to take his friend's place as spokesman for the troops. Despite his resolve, he could not help feeling

A postcard of the North Bay, sent from Scarborough by a holidaymaker in July 1918. The message on the back reads: 'haveing a nice time lovely weather wet all day not many people here plenty of room plenty of meat here'.

South Bay, Scarborough: an old postcard of the Spa building, with its promenaders, and the sands.

'Eat Less Bread': a Food Economy poster. Owen quotes the slogan in 'The Calls'.

bitter towards people who were still able to enjoy a comfortable life, especially the holidaymakers idling on the beaches in this fifth August of the war. Another boat had been sunk that morning.

> I wish the Bosche would have the pluck to come right in & make a clean sweep of the Pleasure Boats, and the promenaders on the Spa, and all the stinking Leeds & Bradford War-profiteers now reading *John Bull* on Scarborough Sands.

His unfinished poem, 'The Calls', reflects his feelings:

> I see a food-hog whet his gold-filled tusk
> To eat less bread, and more luxurious rusk . . .
> I heard the sighs of men, that have no skill
> To speak of their distress, no, nor the will!
> A voice I know. And this time I must go.

Events happened fast and they are not fully recorded. There was little time to write letters (some may have been subsequently 'lost'). Sassoon lost his own diary for this period. On the evening of Sunday 11 August,

Owen wrote to Scott Moncrieff that the medical examination had turned out unexpectedly: 'I was struck off the draft by the M.O. this morning. He won't pass my cardiac valves. . . Yes, I got myself put on the draft list of 22 officers, but couldn't work it this time.' His heart valves had given cause for concern at Dunsden and Ripon. Whether there was really anything wrong with them can only be a matter for speculation. He shared his mother's proneness to hypochondria and some of his pre-war ailments seem to have been psychosomatic. On the other hand, he lived in an age when doctors understood heart noises less well than they do now. Gunston's 'mitral murmur' was no doubt genuine, yet he lived to be over ninety.

Had Owen passed the medical, he would have been entitled to the usual draft leave. As it was, he was due for leave anyway and seems to have been able to go to Shrewsbury, probably on the Monday, arriving unannounced. Both his brothers were away, Harold in Portsmouth and Colin, now in the RAF, in Hastings. With all three of her sons at risk, Mrs Owen was giving full rein to her various illnesses, real and imaginary. Owen recommended red wine as a tonic. She had brought up her children to be abstainers and was alarmed that he might be falling into bad habits. 'You are too absurd!' he told her afterwards, sending her money for half a dozen bottles.

He seems to have been in London by Wednesday 14 August, when Scott Moncrieff gave him a copy of Sacheverell Sitwell's latest poems, and on the Thursday he and Sassoon dined with Meiklejohn at the Reform Club. The medical officer's decision had given Scott Moncrieff the chance to resubmit Owen's name for an instructorship. Owen must have told Sassoon about this and about the draft, because Sassoon said in a letter to Marsh that Thursday that he was greatly relieved that 'someone' had intervened to stop Owen from going to the front after all.[8] (Actually what was stopping Owen from being sent overseas was the doctor's decision; the instructorship application would not have been approved if he had been declared fit for draft.)

Osbert Sitwell and Sassoon remembered Owen as serenely happy on the Saturday afternoon in Chelsea. Sitwell was host and had planned a perfect occasion. Knowing that his guests were passionately fond of music, he took them on a prearranged visit to Violet Gordon Woodhouse, a celebrated performer on the harpsichord. Elegant as 'some exquisite eighteenth-century marquise', she gave them a private concert for over two hours; according to Sitwell, Owen sat 'dazed with

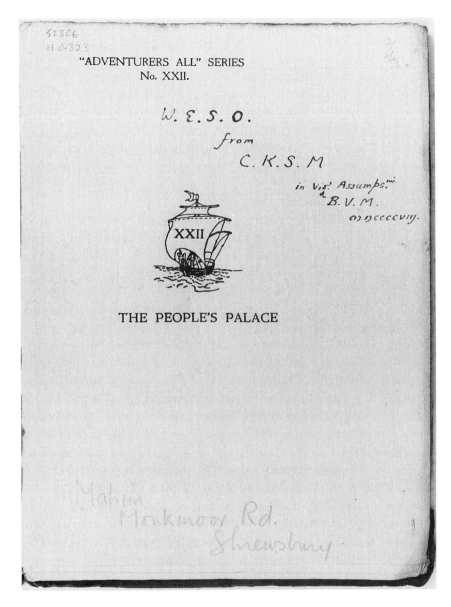

"ADVENTURERS ALL" SERIES
No. XXII.

W. E. S. O.

from

C. K. S. M

in Vig. Assumps.
B. V. M.
ɷ ɲ ccccvɪɪɟ.

XXII

THE PEOPLE'S PALACE

Owen's copy of Sacheverell Sitwell, *The People's Palace*, 1918, inscribed by Scott Moncrieff on 14 August (the Vigil of the Assumption). Owen has added his address, perhaps because he took the book to France.

'Mr Osbert and Mr Sacheverell Sitwell': cartoon by Max Beerbohm. Owen met both brothers in 1918 and saw Beerbohm at Graves's wedding in January ('when he looked at me, I felt my nose tip-tilting in an alarming manner; my legs warped; my chin became a mere pimple on my neck').

happiness at the fire and audacity of the player'. Afterwards they returned to Sitwell's house in Swan Walk for 'a sumptuous tea', Sassoon recalled, 'which culminated in – was it raspberries and cream? – and ices of incredibly creamy quality'. Then they crossed the road to the old, walled Physic Garden, to which Sitwell had a key, and sat in the sun. 'It was the ideal of a summer afternoon', according to Sitwell:

> various shrubs, late-flowering magnolias and the like, were in blossom, there was a shimmer and flutter in the upper leaves, and a perfection of contentment and peacefulness, unusual in the tense atmosphere of a hot day in London, especially during a war, breathed over the scene. So listlessly happy was Owen that he could not bring himself to leave the Garden to go to the station and catch the train he had arranged to take.[9]

In the end Sassoon had to return to Lancaster Gate, so Owen went with him. They shook hands on the steps of the hospital. Owen mumbled something about wanting to go out again, and Sassoon said it might be a good thing for his poetry but he would stab him in the leg first.[10] Three days later Sassoon left for a nursing home in Scotland, visiting Craiglockhart to see Rivers on the way. He found the 'accursed place' as depressing as ever.

The send-off

Owen got back to camp on the Saturday evening. This time he was patrol officer and had to spend the Sunday night out on duty. He enjoyed it, especially watching the dawn come up over the sea, but he had an attack of trench foot afterwards (a stress symptom?) and was unable to walk. By the time he wrote to his mother (twice) on the Monday (19 August) he seems to have known that he was destined for France. His evening letter from the tent aches with homesickness. 'I am quite wretched tonight, missing you so much. Oh so much!' His 'excellent little servant Jones', the only person in Scarborough he could feel certain of, was prattling away in an attempt to cheer him up, '& I am talking volubly while I write. / I am also thinking wildly and crying a little for only you to hear'.

No letters survive for the next eleven days, although he must have written some. He may have found that he was being talked about. After his sporting activities in previous weeks, the bridge players in the mess would have been derisive about his suspect heart valves, especially if they knew that another attempt had been made to get him a safe job. What he had meant to be an honourable return to active service had begun to look like shirking.

The renewed application for an instructorship had in fact been turned down. As Scott Moncrieff later recorded, the decision was made 'on the ground that the state of health in which [Owen] had come home a year earlier implied a shock to and consequent weakening of his *moral*, and that such "cases" were not to be put in positions, in any way privileged, at home'. Scott Moncrieff saw the original memorandum but did not quote it; the words did 'not look well in print'. Colonel Mitchell may have been sent copies of the official correspondence. It is difficult to resist the suspicion that he had a word with the medical officer. On the 26th the adjutant reissued the embarkation order, noting that the doctor had now certified that Owen was fit to proceed overseas.[11]

Owen settled up his mess bill with Major Fletcher that day and seems to have left at once on brief draft leave. Jones had been standing by for days to pack his things 'in quarter of an hour, night or day'. The folders of verse manuscripts were probably put in last of all, as Owen had been struggling to copy out some poems for *Wheels*. Presumably there was a final visit to Shrewsbury, when the folders were stowed away in the

```
SUBJECT:- Embarkation Orders.
         ..................
TO:-
        2/Lieut. W.E.S.Owen,
        5th (Res) Bn.Manchester Regt.

        With reference to your Embarkation Orders for France,
   the Medical Officer now certifies that you are fit to proceed
   overseas.  In accordance with War Office Letter 5649/6
   (M.S.1.R) para.1. dated 17/9/17, you are therefore instructed
   to report to the Embarkation Commandant, Folkestone, on
   Saturday next, the 31st inst. before 10.0 a.m. and if passing
   through London, you should travel by the train leaving
   Victoria Station at 7.35 a.m. on that date.
        Your attention is directed to para.3 of the copy of
   your original instructions.

   Barracks,
   SCARBOROUGH.                              Captain & Adjutant,
   26th Aug.1918.         5th (Res.) BN. MANCHESTER REGIMENT.
```

The second embarkation order, 26 August.

attic room. Only a year earlier, he had been working on 'The Dead-Beat' in the first excitement of meeting Sassoon. Now he had well over thirty war poems that he knew were good. If anything happened to him, Sassoon and the Sitwells would see to publication. One can imagine him fussing over papers until the last minute, scribbling revisions. He had never been good at being punctual.

By the 30th he was at Hastings with his mother and Colin. Gazing across the Channel, he quoted from Tagore: 'When I go from hence let this be my parting word, that what I have seen is unsurpassable'. He had quoted the same line in 1917 after Beaumont Hamel. Whatever happened, he was determined that things should be better now. He returned to London alone and very late, his train 'enormously delayed' by a royal visit. Scott Moncrieff met him at Victoria.

Finding no porter, Owen helped himself to a trolley and wheeled his luggage to a hotel he had in mind. No room was available. Scott Moncrieff was in a bad temper after the long wait.

I was sickened by the failure to keep him in England, and savage with my own unhealed wounds and the unending competition to work and eat and live in London. If I was harsh with him, may I be forgiven,

Susan, Colin, and Wilfred
Owen were photographed
together at Hastings. Mrs
Owen later had this portrait
made from the print.

as we tramped wearily round the overflowing hotels. In the end a bed
was found in Eaton Square, and we sat down to a strange supper in
the Queen Mary Hut . . . After a few intense hours of books and talk in
my lodging [in Cadogan Square], I escorted him to his. As we reached
it, he discovered that he had left his stick behind, but insisted that it
was too late now to return. I left him on the doorstep and went home
to find, not only the stick but his pocket-book with, I suppose, all his
money, on my table. I went back with them, but I hope he was
already asleep.

As usual, Scott Moncrieff hints at more than he says. If he suggested
that Owen should share his lodging for the night rather than tramp the
streets, his offer would have been refused. Owen described the evening
in a letter home, almost all of which is 'missing'.

Owen got up at 5.30 next morning, in good time for the 7.35 train to
Folkestone. He was astonished and pleased to meet Major Fletcher, who
had been 'pushed off' from Scarborough only a day after his own
departure. They reported to the embarkation commandant on the
quay, to be told that the boat would leave at 3 p.m. Jones was no doubt
in attendance, and could be left in charge of the luggage. Owen slipped
away to get a shave. Then he went down to the beach, expecting to feel
depressed.

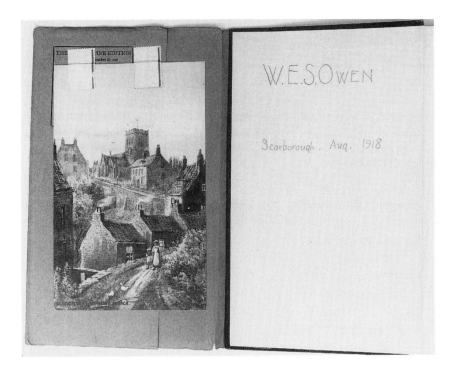

Owen's copy of Swinburne, *Poems and Ballads (First Series)*. The postcard shows St Mary's, Scarborough, seen from the castle. Susan Owen later wrote on the flap: 'This came back with his things from France'.

But I was too happy, or the Sun was too supreme. Moreover, there issued from the sea distraction, in the shape, Shape I say, but lay no stress on that, of a Harrow boy, of superb intellect & refinement; intellect because he hates war more than the Germans; refinement because of the way he spoke of my Going, and of the Sun, and of the Sea there; and the way he spoke of Everything. In fact, the way he spoke –

That description to Sassoon was repeated almost verbatim to Mrs Owen, with the prudent omission of the bit about 'Shape'. It was a strange meeting, almost like finding one's ideal self.

RETURN TO FRANCE

Base

As soon as he arrived at Boulogne on the last day of August 1918, Owen wrote home and sent a note to Sassoon, who imagined him to be still safely in Yorkshire.

Goodbye –
    dear Siegfried –
I'm much nearer to you here than in Scarborough, and am by so much happier.

I have been incoherent ever since I tried to say goodbye on the steps of Lancaster Gate. But everything is clear now: & I'm in hasty retreat towards the Front. Battle is easier here; and therefore you will stay and endure old men & women to the End, and wage the bitterer war and more hopeless. . . .

What more is there to say that you will not better understand unsaid.

As in December 1916, he was sent first to the base camp at Etaples, a short rail journey down the coast. He had described the place as a 'vast, dreadful encampment', 'a kind of paddock where the beasts are kept a few days before the shambles'. The image had remained with him ('these who die as cattle') and now he told Sassoon: 'I am among the herds again, a Herdsman; and a Shepherd of sheep that do not know my voice'. Troops were never at Etaples long enough to know anyone's voice. By day they were put through a short course of intensive training and gas drills to prepare them for the real thing, and by night they were penned in huge depots behind barbed wire. Then they were allocated to units in the line and sent away on crowded trains, sometimes in cattle trucks. For a few days in September 1917 the herds refused to obey orders. That produced improvements.[1] Owen found the place 'vastly

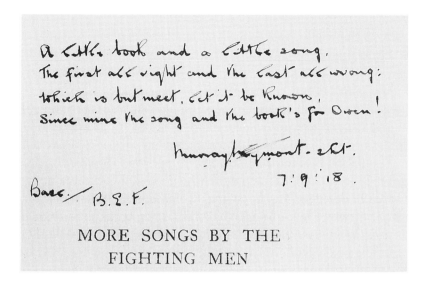

A little book and a little song,
The first all right and the last all wrong:
Which is but meet, let it be known,
Since mine the song and the book's for Owen!

Murray McClymont - 2Lt.

7:9:18.

Base: / B.E.F.

MORE SONGS BY THE
FIGHTING MEN

Murray McClymont's inscription in the copy of the anthology *Soldier Poets*,
which he gave to Owen on 7 September.

more habitable' than it had been. He still had to marshal unknown
men, but he slept in a hut instead of a tent and there was plenty of free
time. His previous visit had been in the depths of winter, with snow
blowing in from the sea; in the hot September sun the dunes and stunted
pines looked much less cruel.

He was determined to keep his spirits up. Not for him the 'dead rabbit'
look he had seen on men's faces in Etaples at the end of 1916. 'You
would not know me for the poet of sorrows.' Two people who met him at
the camp remembered him as friendly and good-humoured. One was
Second Lieutenant Murray McClymont, who was introduced as a
fellow-poet, having contributed to a popular anthology. Owen thought
little of his poems but found the 'big Scotchman' 'useful as an audience',
and they spent a convivial evening together, talking of Sassoon. The
other new acquaintance was more interesting, 'an extraordinary
hunch-backed little Irishman, of very pleasant manners'.[2]

Conal O'Riordan, whose name Owen vaguely knew, was a novelist
and playwright, a friend of Yeats, Synge, and other famous writers, and
a former director of the Abbey Theatre in Dublin. He had volunteered for
overseas work earlier in the year, even though he was middle aged and

badly crippled from a boyhood riding accident (he was invalided home as soon as the war ended). Since August he had been responsible for a YMCA rest hut at the railway station, braving air raids and watching over an endless succession of young officers as they slept under his roof for a few hours before he woke them for their trains.

Owen found him alone in the hut one afternoon and thereafter called in almost daily. O'Riordan said later that of all the thousands of men he encountered in Etaples, he could remember 'no cheerier companion or blither soul than the charming young Wilfred Owen'. 'I see so clearly his charming face; a child's, despite the tiny moustache, smiling at me in the sunlight or under the rays of the swinging lamp he would light for me when I drew the curtains at evenfall.' They talked for hours, 'not books', as Owen said, 'but life & people, as is the way between Authors'.

Owen explained his convictions about the war, saying the Allies were as much to blame as Germany. O'Riordan considered this dangerous heresy, pointing out that as an Irishman himself he had no cause to be well disposed towards the British, yet here he was, doing what he could to help defeat 'the crazy beast of Hohenzollernism'. He thought Owen's conversation ranged from 'the most beauteous and humane wisdom', when they shared their hatred of killing and newspaper rhetoric, to 'what I warned him was . . . comprehensible but not the less unbalanced and intellectually indefensible folly'. It seemed that Owen was partly persuaded, but he did not show O'Riordan his poems.

The rest hut was a welcome refuge from the main camp, where there were still some officers from the Scarborough draft whom Owen had not wished to see again. He asked the camp authorities if he could transfer to a Welsh regiment. It would be good to make a new start, and perhaps his Welsh ancestry would help his soldiering; he had always believed it had helped to make him a poet. However, he was told to join the 2nd Manchesters and think himself lucky. This was the Regular battalion he had been with in 1917. At least he would get away from 'the Scarborough mob'.

On Sunday 8 September he assembled a party of troops, none of whom knew him, for the train journey to Amiens. Just as they were moving off, 'a private rushed out from the crowd' and wished him luck: it was a man who remembered him from 1916. 'The augury was good, and I think the incident put my draft in a confident mood.' They arrived in Amiens in the dark and the herdsman had to wait for guides before he could deliver his charges, who 'behaved excellently', evidently

Right: The south transept of Amiens Cathedral, seen through ruined houses, June 1918.

Below: Amiens Cathedral, sandbagged against the shelling in April 1918.

appreciative of his care.

His own billet was in a large, shell-damaged house, where he had to share a room with a young second lieutenant named Potts, 'a good solid companion, not without wit, & full of wisdom'. Nearly a week passed in 'reading, sleeping [on a table], conversing, & gathering roses from bewildered gardens'. Many civilians had fled in the April shelling. The two subalterns hunted for furniture and souvenirs, kicking about in the shattered houses and rubble-strewn streets. Near the cathedral, Owen picked up 'a delightful wee lace-surplice', an appropriate souvenir for an Aesthete.

One afternoon he 'took a joy ride in a tank' and on another revisited the Somme canal at Cerisy and again remembered the hospital barges. The area had been recaptured on 8 August, a day which later came to be seen as the start of the final Allied victory. There were plenty of scars left from that battle and from the German offensive in March-April. If he went to look at the great church at Corbie not far away, where he had listened in vain for 'the voice of the Middle Ages' in 1917, he would have found it roofless. He paused at an Australian YMCA, 'a shack of a cottage', and used some of its writing paper to revise a few poems.

The resolute emphasis on enjoyment, serenity, and good health, which is such a conspicuous feature of his letters from France, was not

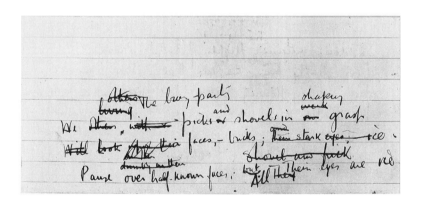

Owen's editors have had to reconstruct the last stanza of 'Exposure' from these scribbles on a double sheet of paper, the end of a hasty draft probably made at Amiens in September 1918. His first three editors (Sassoon, Blunden, Day Lewis) read 'His frost' for 'this frost'. No one has been able to explain his curious date, unless he meant to write 'Feb 1918', possibly the date of the first complete draft (now lost).

only intended to reassure his mother and Sassoon. It was also a means of self-discipline; 'still I say Will is the best medicine', he said in October, in answer to yet more of Mrs Owen's complaints about her health. Brock had told him many times that nervous trouble could be prevented by the efficient use of will-power. One did not have to let oneself be depressed by ruined houses, nor by the wet, cold weather that was now bringing in the autumn. It was good to be in the right place, with the Army in France. He thought of his brothers, both in uniform, and asked his mother to tell them, 'and them only, how peculiarly unreluctant I am . . . to have the Channel between me and all that the Gunstons typify'.

With the old battalion

The 'amusing little holiday' in Amiens ended on Friday 13 September. The brigade was being withdrawn after some heavy fighting, and Owen

Therefore, not loathe, we lie out here; therefore were born,
For love of God seems dying.
Tonight, frost will fasten on this mud and us,
Shrivelling many hands, and puckering foreheads crisp.
The burying-party, picks and shovels in their shaking grasp,
Pause over half-known faces. All their eyes are ice,
But nothing happens.

Feb. 1918.

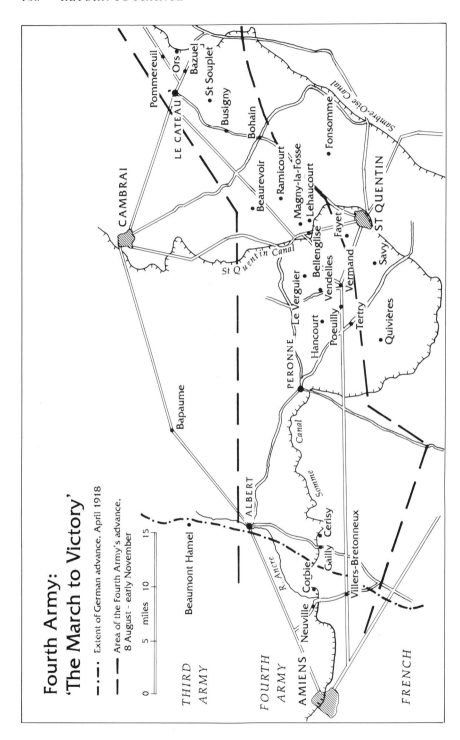

Fourth Army:
'The March to Victory'

· — · — · Extent of German advance, April 1918

———— Area of the Fourth Army's advance,
8 August - early November

0   5   10   15
|————|————|————|
        miles

had to help arrange billets. He watched the Manchesters 'march in' next day and was pleased to be recognized by two men as they went by, rare survivors from his previous time at the front. At 9 a.m. on the Sunday, he, Potts, Second Lieutenant Foulkes, and three others reported to the adjutant in the area of La Neuville, near Corbie.

The 96th Infantry Brigade consisted of three infantry battalions (2nd Manchesters and 15th and 16th Lancashire Fusiliers), supported by 218 Field Company Royal Engineers, and trench mortar and machine gun units. A battalion was normally divided into four companies, each with a company sergeant-major, and a company into four platoons, each with a platoon sergeant. A platoon at full strength (as many were not by 1918) contained about thirty-five men. At the other end of the scale, the brigade was one of the three in the 32nd Division, which in turn was one of the four divisions in the Fourth Army's IX Corps. The Fourth Army was fighting east of Amiens, its battalions 'leap-frogging' each other as the front advanced, following a routine of rest-reserve-support-lead-rest.

Owen was put in charge of 16 Platoon in D Company, under a Captain Somerville, and realized that the other three company officers, John Foulkes among them, were his juniors. They soon took to calling him 'The Ghost', either because he had been rumoured to be dead or because he kept himself as inconspicuous as usual. Foulkes thought him 'a thorough gentleman', though, 'courteous to all ranks – willing and eager to help anybody. I always suspected him of having an extra soft spot for Tommy, although he never allowed it to interfere with discipline. Whilst seeming to thoroughly understand the soldier's attitude to most things he himself seemed to me to have a curious lack of growl.' Foulkes never guessed that Owen was a poet, although he once heard him discussing Sassoon with Somerville and often saw him reading a little volume of Swinburne. Somerville was an Edinburgh graduate and agreeably literary.

As always in new billets, the battalion devoted its first day to 'general clean-up' of premises and equipment. The men were paid. Owen went to Battalion HQ to look for letters, until a 'Terrible Major' asked him what he wanted and he hastily departed. (Major J.N. Marshall, ten times wounded and often decorated, was the sort of 'arrant utterly soldierly soldier' one did well to avoid. Fortunately the colonel was a 'mild, honourable gentleman'.) At 5 p.m. there was a voluntary service (C. of E.). Owen may well have attended; apostate though he still was, he loved the old words and had often been to services at Ripon and elsewhere during the year.

There followed days of what the Army was pleased to call 'rest'. On the Monday, stores and kit were checked and the men were sent to the divisional bath-house for three hours of scrubbing, delousing, and a change of clothes. D Company took its daily turn at physical training, the Lewis gun, musketry, and compulsory games. Every now and then there was a sudden gas drill, and the divisional gas officer gave two lectures. Owen was made battalion bombing officer, although he knew 'nothing specially about bombs'; the adjutant seemed to think him a useful man.

On 19 September *The Times* published a crude translation of a speech by Clemenceau to the French Senate. Still determined to be 'fully satisfied', the old 'Tiger' had been reaffirming his belief in the need for complete victory. Anything less would be a betrayal of the dead. It was just the sort of thing that would have driven Sassoon to write a satire in 1917. As his substitute, Owen wrote a satire himself, using phrases from *The Times* report.

> '. . . We rulers sitting in this ancient spot
> Would wrong our very selves if we forgot
> The greatest glory will be theirs who fought,
> Who kept this nation in integrity.'
> Nation? – The half-limbed readers did not chafe
> But smiled at one another curiously
> Like secret men who know their secret safe.
> (This is the thing they know and never speak,
> That England one by one had fled to France,
> Not many elsewhere now, save under France.)

Owen's ironic comment echoes an earlier remark that he was glad to be back 'with *the Nation*' in France. The poet of sorrows, who was also a poet of secrets, knew that there was a bond within 'the Nation Overseas' which most of 'the Nation at Home' would never understand. (There were a few exceptions, such as the Harrow boy.) He sent a copy of 'Smile, Smile, Smile' to Sassoon on the 22nd, also enclosing a final draft of 'The Sentry', which he had begun a year earlier at Craiglockhart, and part of 'Spring Offensive', a new poem probably started in the summer.

The last lines of 'Spring Offensive' must have been written after the

Owen's last complete poem: a draft of 'Smile, Smile, Smile', on the back of a letter from McClymont.

22nd.[3] They are his final comment on his chosen subject, 'War, and the pity of War', and they reflect the mood of the men around him. The Manchesters had done well in recent weeks. Long lists of awards came through. Somerville got a bar to his MC. A brigadier-general watched the battalion drilling on the 26th and complimented it on its 'excellent work' at the front. The newspapers were full of praise for the latest successes. The men who had done the fighting were less forthcoming, knowing what it meant to kill and see one's friends killed; they had survived, by chance, and they remembered comrades who had not.

> But what say such as from existence' brink
> Ventured but drave too swift to sink,
> The few who rushed in the body to enter hell,
> And there out-fiending all its fiends and flames
> With superhuman inhumanities,
> Long-famous glories, immemorial shames –
> And crawling slowly back, have by degrees
> Regained cool peaceful air in wonder –
> Why speak not they of comrades that went under?

Owen wanted 'Spring Offensive' to be intelligible to soldiers; only they would see the point of his final question.

Moving up

On 24 September the battalion began yet another move towards the line, 'embussing' on the road from Corbie to Villers-Bretonneux, ten miles east of Amiens. Villers was famous as the furthest point reached by the German advance in April. No one could know that during the next few weeks the brigade was going to cross the whole width of the wrecked landscape where war had ebbed and flowed for four years, and emerge on the far side into open country where there were still villages and even villagers. The first leg of the journey was the easiest, the transport lurching slowly along the Roman road that runs due east from Amiens towards St Quentin.

The battalion 'debussed' for four days of exercises near Tertry in the 'forward area', well within the wasteland left by the Germans during their withdrawal to the Hindenburg Line in the spring of 1917. Villages had been destroyed, woods cut down, wells blocked, roads mined, and everywhere there were old trenches and wire. The damage had

Owen may have seen this sign on
the Amiens–St Quentin road.
Originally British, it was added to by
the Germans in their 1918 advance
and again by the Australians,
whose photographer recorded it on
13 September.

hampered the Germans' own advance in March–April 1918. Since
August the Allies had been driving them back over the same ground.
While Owen was at Tertry, French troops reached 'Manchester Hill' and
Savy Wood in front of St Quentin, where he had been through the
artillery barrage remembered in 'Spring Offensive'. It was a war of
movement now, and in the blasted fields around the camp the battalion
reverted to the old nineteenth-century drills, once automatic to every
British soldier, of moving from column to line and attacking a strong
point.

At midday on Saturday 28 September, Owen sat on some straw in his
'Tamboo' (probably a corrugated iron shelter), out of the rain, waiting
for Jones to bring him his lunch. He wrote home as cheerfully as he
could.

These few days have been dry & not really cold. You must not suppose
I have been uncomfortable. Though I left the last vestige of
civilization, in the Civil sense, behind at ---, there is here all but all
that a man wants fundamentally; clean air, enough water to wash
once a day; plain food and plentiful; letters from Home of good news,
shelter from the rain & cold; an intellectual gentleman for Captain; 3
bright & merry boys for my corporals; & stout grizzled old soldiers in

A typical village in the devastated zone: the ruins of Le Verguier on 24 September. The Manchesters passed through five days later.

my platoon. . . .

Here is my lunch; roast beef & baked potatoes! I'm hungry!

That was the best he could do to reassure his mother. He did not mention that in the east the guns had been roaring in unison since the previous evening. Planes droned overhead, and the landscape was alive with troops and transport moving up to the front. The last great battle of the war was about to begin.

From Tertry onwards, progress would have to be on foot. The brigade set out on the first of its route marches that evening. Orders were precise, as always: a hundred yards between companies, five hundred between battalions, packs to be worn. The men were to keep fit and fresh; if they halted, they were to take off their equipment and lie down, not stand under arms or wander about. The Manchesters started at 7.38 p.m., avoiding the crowded roads by following lanes and a field track through Poeuilly and Soyécourt. They were all present in a field near Vendelles by 9.50. 'Bivouacs' were waiting for them, tents and iron shelters (this new kind of war allowed no time for the old routine of 'digging in').

Breaking the Hindenburg Line

No one fully realized until afterwards that from 8 August onwards the final 'Hundred Days' were a continuous success, a 'March to Victory'. Even in late September the Hindenburg Line still lay ahead. Built to be impregnable, it was the most formidable barrier that human ingenuity had yet devised, an intricate, miles-deep network of wire, trenches, gun pits, tunnels, redoubts, and concrete machine gun posts (pill boxes). Nowhere was the defence stronger than in the so-called 'Siegfried Stellung' immediately north of St Quentin, opposite the Fourth Army. Here the St Quentin canal had been strengthened as a moat, in front of elaborate fortifications. Two miles or so beyond these lay a 'Support Line' and about three miles beyond that again a strong 'Reserve Line'.

Once the Allies had reached the outer defences, they decided to try for a massive breakthrough before the enemy had time to get established. The assault began on 27 September along many miles of front. In the Fourth Army's sector, the artillery put down a gas barrage all night and then heavy shells – over a million of them – for two days. On the morning of the 29th, three Staffordshire battalions led the 46th Division forward, making a superb crossing of the canal between Riqueval and Bellenglise. They dropped into the steep cutting and swam across in life jackets sent up from the Channel ferries, moving so fast that the enemy had no time to blow up the last of the bridges. The rest of the division poured across, taking the defenders by surprise, and the 32nd followed, ready to leap-frog into the lead. Men who crossed the canal that afternoon saw the signs of success: bridges under construction, troops and guns going forward, parties of prisoners being taken to the rear. By the evening the engineers had even restored electric light to the tunnels.

The 96th Brigade, which was in reserve, set out from Vendelles in the afternoon through the wrecked village of Le Verguier, crossing the canal and passing through the triumphant 46th Division. The Manchesters brought up the rear after dark, spending the night in

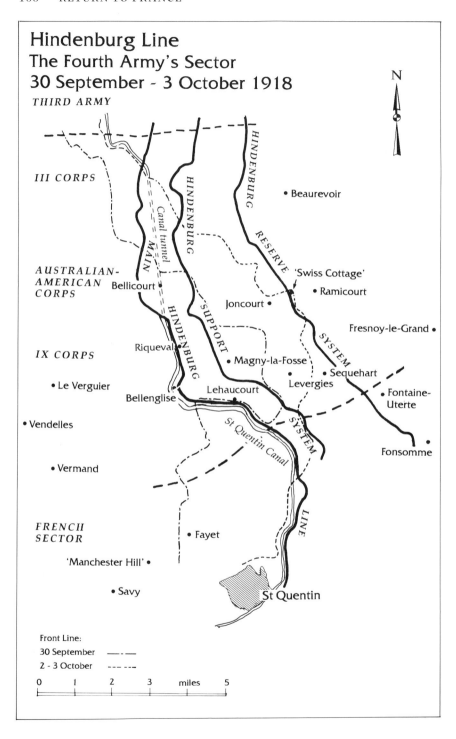

Hindenburg Line
The Fourth Army's Sector
30 September - 3 October 1918

N

THIRD ARMY

III CORPS

• Beaurevoir

Canal tunnel

HINDENBURG MAIN

HINDENBURG

HINDENBURG

RESERVE

AUSTRALIAN-
AMERICAN   Bellicourt •
CORPS

'Swiss Cottage'

• Ramicourt

SUPPORT

Joncourt •

SYSTEM

Fresnoy-le-Grand •

IX CORPS

Riqueval •

HINDENBURG

• Magny-la-Fosse

• Le Verguier

Lehaucourt

Levergies

• Sequehart

Bellenglise

• Fontaine-
Uterte

• Vendelles

St Quentin Canal

SYSTEM

Fonsomme

• Vermand

LINE

FRENCH
SECTOR

• Fayet

'Manchester Hill' •

• Savy

St Quentin

Front Line:

30 September —.—

2 - 3 October --- ---

0   1   2   3   miles   5

newly-captured trenches in the Support Line, just west of Magny-la-Fosse. Next day the brigade caught up with the front, suffering its first casualties, and reached a railway cutting south of Joncourt. On the morning of 1 October the 15th Lancashire Fusiliers turned north to help capture the village, while the Manchesters took up positions in front of a far more strongly held objective, the Hindenburg Reserve Line itself, known in this sector as the Beaurevoir-Fonsomme Line.

The modern image of the First World War as a futile stalemate has tended to obscure the nature of its closing battles. The 2nd Manchesters, many of them teenagers, had marched for miles over difficult ground in cold, wet weather. They had probably had no hot food since leaving Vendelles. There were no 'friendly' trenches or other forms of shelter. The deceptively open landscape was full of invisible machine guns, and heavy artillery shelled incessantly from behind the hills. Gas masks often had to be put on in a hurry. Ahead, on the crest of a ridge, immense thickets of wire stretched north and south as far as the eye could see, protecting a hidden line of pill boxes and gun pits.

The battalion had the task of capturing about 1400 yards of the Beaurevoir-Fonsomme Line, south from a building marked on the

Troops and a tank advancing towards the Hindenburg Line on 29 September.

Divisional maps as 'Swiss Cottage'. C and D Companies were to lead. Zero hour was 4 p.m., to be timed on Owen's watch. Four tanks arrived, having got across the canal after severe delays, and planes patrolled overhead. If a plane sounded a klaxon, troops were to show their positions by firing flares. With the approach of zero, a barrage of shrapnel, smoke, and machine gun fire opened up against the ridge and then, even before the whistles blew for the infantry to advance up the hill, three of the tanks were put out of action (one later got going again).[4]

The loss of the tanks, which were to have gone forward with the troops, may have caused a delay. In the next hour Jones was hit in the head, falling on top of the officer whose life he was protecting. He lay there for half an hour, with his head on Owen's shoulder. ('Catalogue? Photograph? Can you photograph the crimson-hot iron as it cools from the smelting? That is what Jones's blood looked like, and felt like. My senses are charred.') Somerville was wounded in the thigh, and of the D Company officers only Foulkes and Owen were left unhurt.

Soaked in Jones's blood, and accompanied by a 'seraphic' boy lance-corporal in place of a sergeant-major, Owen found himself leading not a platoon but a company.[5] He did not record exactly what happened.

> I can find no word to qualify my experiences except the word SHEER. . . It passed the limits of my Abhorrence. I lost all my earthly faculties, and fought like an angel.
>
> If I started into detail of our engagement I should disturb the censor and my own Rest.

It seems that the angel and the seraph captured a pill box and a machine gun. According to the citation for the Military Cross which Owen was later awarded, he 'personally manipulated' the gun 'from an isolated position', inflicting 'considerable losses on the enemy'. (In his letter home he only said he had shot one man with his revolver.) The rest of the battalion was in the German line, fighting at close quarters. Through the rattle of gunfire and the crash of the shells came the steady roar of five more tanks moving up. The defence wavered and broke. Owen held 'a most glorious brief peace talk' in the pill box. Over 200 men surrendered, bringing with them 24 machine guns. By about 6.30 p.m. the attack was over.

With the battle still going on round them, the Manchesters

The Manchesters crossed this stretch of the St Quentin canal on 29 September. The view is south towards Bellenglise from the bridge at Riqueval on 2 October; Staffordshires are dispersing after being congratulated by their CO.

Wire and the shallow trench, Beaurevoir-Fonsomme (Hindenburg Reserve) Line, 10 October 1918.

consolidated their new position. Their success deserved to become a 'long-famous glory', although it was in fact destined to be only a few lines in the history books. In effect C and D Companies were the spearhead of the Fourth Army, having outpaced all flanking units and become the only Allied troops to break into the last line of the

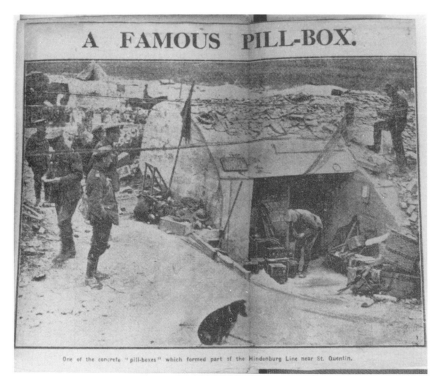

A FAMOUS PILL-BOX.

One of the concrete " pill-boxes " which formed part of the Hindenburg Line near St. Quentin.

An unidentified cutting in a scrapbook kept by Tom Owen. The pill box
captured by his son probably looked much like this one.

Hindenburg system. It was a horribly dangerous place to be. The
battalion was heavily outnumbered, and the enemy was bringing up
reinforcements. The village of Ramicourt ahead was strongly held.
Enfilading fire came from a wood on the right, while the Australian-
American corps on the left was still so far behind that Swiss Cottage was
exposed on three sides (hence Owen's *double entendre* to Sassoon later: 'I
desire no more *exposed flanks* of any sort for a long time').

The Germans had never quite finished the Reserve Line: there were
pits three or four feet deep for riflemen and machine gunners, but the
connecting trench was only a foot deep and vulnerable to fire from what
had been its rear. Owen set up his base in the captured pill box (while he
was there a note arrived from Scott Moncrieff, proof of the remarkable
efficiency of the military postal service). The pill box probably had to be

evacuated, being all too obvious a target. During the night, officers and men together 'lay in the mud utterly despondent'. Luckily a lance-corporal had ignored regulations and brought a blanket, which he shared with his commander: 'the warmth came like the rising of the May Day sun'.

A party of Lancashire Fusiliers managed to bring up rations, and later a company from their 15th Battalion reached the line to help with the defence. The enemy launched repeated counter-attacks. Swiss Cottage changed hands several times, and in the hand-to-hand fighting there Foulkes personally rushed a machine-gun, killing its crew; a strong patrol under his leadership finally secured the place, capturing eighteen Germans and several machine guns.

All night and for hours next day the wounded lay groaning just out of reach. Three stretcher bearers went to help and were hit one after the other. 'I had to order no one to show himself after that', Owen wrote afterwards,

> but remembering my own duty, and remembering also my fore-fathers the agile Welshmen of the Mountains I scrambled out myself & felt an exhilaration in baffling the Machine Guns by quick bounds from cover to cover. After the shells we had been through, and the gas, bullets were like the gentle rain from heaven.

Progress was impossible. The 16th Lancashires tried to take Ramicourt but were driven back, and an attempt by the Argyll and Sutherland Highlanders to capture the section of trench south of the Manchesters' position was also repulsed. In the rear, detachments of cavalry waited in vain for the great charge the generals had ordered them to expect. No unit in the Fourth Army was able to move forward that day.

Battalion casualties on 1 October, the day of the attack, were 4 other ranks killed, 78 wounded, and 7 missing; 6 officers were wounded, including Potts, and one was killed (Owen had known him in Scarborough and commented, 'I suppose [his] child will be told she should be proud of Daddie, now'). The rate of losses for officers suggests that Owen was not exaggerating his own exploits: subalterns were expected to lead from the front. By contrast, only one officer became a casualty on 2–3 October, when 23 other ranks were killed, 70 wounded, and 20 recorded as missing. Some of the losses were from gas; in spite of all the practice drills, men were too slow with their masks.

Entrances to German dug-outs on the banks of the St Quentin canal, 4 October.

The 32nd Division had achieved as much as could be expected of it, and during the night the 46th once again took over the lead. At five in the morning on 3 October, Owen used his knowledge of astronomy and 'led the Company out, by the stars, through an air mysterious with faint gas'. 'This is where I admired his work', Foulkes remembered, 'in leading his remnants, in the middle of the night, back to safety . . . I was content to follow him with the utmost confidence in his leadership'. The battalion was withdrawn to German shelters on the wooded canal banks near Lehaucourt.

In London that day, Sassoon was introduced to Winston Churchill, who showed a surprising admiration for his poems, offered him a job in the Ministry of Munitions, and expatiated on war's value as an instrument for social and scientific progress. In the evening, Sassoon dined with Maynard Keynes, saw the Sitwells, and called in at Half Moon Street, hoping for a few quiet hours. The calm was broken by the arrival of Scott Moncrieff, whom Sassoon detested, and an effusive youth named Noel Coward. When Sassoon rose to go, Ross followed him to the door and held his hand for a moment. It was their last meeting. On the 5th, Burton found Ross dead from heart failure. Owen heard the news a week later from Scott Moncrieff, who also told him Bainbrigge had been killed. By then Scott Moncrieff had got himself to Amiens as an assistant press officer, responsible for correspondents and photographers. He hoped to see Owen soon.

— 7 —

·THE BATTLE OF THE SAMBRE CANAL

'Such a desent chap'

ON 4 October the battalion returned to Vendelles, and by the following afternoon it was in what Owen described as 'the acute discomfort' of iron shelters at Hancourt, not far from Tertry. The familiar round began again: 'general clean-up', baths, new clothes, church parades. On the 14th the men were entertained by 'The Pedlers' (whoever was keeping the battalion diary was not good at spelling). Companies, platoons, and sections were reorganized to take account of casualties. Training was again for movement: route marching, deployment, consolidation.

Owen was still Acting Captain. That gave him the right to ride a 'Charger', which he enjoyed as a capable horseman. He had been recommended for the Military Cross for his leadership in the attack and was glad, he told Sassoon, 'for the confidence it may give me at home'. His courage, and his authority as a poet, were now beyond question, and like Sassoon he had made the welfare of his men his first concern. To his mother he made a claim which was to become famous: 'I came out in order to help these boys – directly by leading them as well as an officer can; indirectly, by watching their sufferings that I may speak of them as well as a pleader can. I have done the first.' And neurasthenia had not returned. 'My nerves are in perfect order.'

There is a curious remark in his letter to Sassoon: 'I have nothing to tell you except that I'm rather glad my servant was happily wounded: & so away from me. He had lived in London, a Londoner.' The opening words seem to signal a special message (after all, there were plenty of other things to tell Sassoon). Even if Jones was not the Hereford gardener's boy mentioned in a Scarborough letter, he is unlikely to have been a 'Londoner' in a regiment drawn from Lancashire and the Welsh border. Perhaps the term had some special meaning in Ross's circle.[1]

Awarded the Military Cross.

2nd Lieutenant Wilfred Edward Salter Owen,
5th Battalion, Manchester Regiment, T.F., attached 2nd
Battalion.

For conspicuous gallantry and devotion to duty in the attack on the Fonsomme Line on 1st/2nd Oct. 1918. On the Company Commander becoming a casualty, he assumed command and shewed fine leadership and resisted a heavy counter attack. He personally manipulated a captured enemy M.G. from an isolated position and inflicted considerable losses on the enemy.

Throughout he behaved most gallantly.

A copy of the official citation for Owen's Military Cross, preserved in his father's scrapbook.

CITATION

Awarded the Military Cross.

2nd Lieutenant Wilfred Edward Salter Owen,
5th Battalion, Manchester Regiment, T.F. attached 2nd Battalion.

For conspicuous gallantry and devotion to duty in the attack on the Fonsomme Line on 1st/2nd Oct.1918.. On the Company Commander becoming a casualty, he assumed command and shewed fine leadership and resisted a heavy counter attack. He personally captured an enemy Machine Gun in an isolated position and took a number of prisoners.

Throughout he behaved most gallantly.

Another version of the MC citation, found among the family papers and quoted as correct in the *Collected Letters*. Presumably a family forgery: capturing prisoners would have seemed a more appropriate activity for a war poet than inflicting 'considerable losses' with a machine gun.

A big draft arrived from Scarborough on 10 October. Much to Owen's delight, it included some 'outgrown drummers' who had been among his waiters at Clarence Gardens. He noticed that some of them looked 'pretty scared already, poor victims.' Censoring letters soon afterwards he

> came across this: 'Do you know that little officer called Owen who was at Scarborough; he is commanding my Company, and he is a *toff* I can tell you. No na-poo. Compree?' Interpreted: 'a fine fellow, no nonsense about him!'
>
> I record this because it is more pleasing than military medals with many bars.

Another letter said Mr Owen 'his such a desent chap'. He kept his mind firmly on his duties. There was no point yet in thinking about Jones and the poem that could surely be made out of the crimson of his sacrifice, nor about the 'considerable losses' caused by the machine gun. There were endless casualty reports and letters of condolence to be written. Owen chain-smoked, did his job, smiled at the youngsters. Looking at men coughing from gas, he said: 'I am paralysed when I try to write to Leslie: so many of these boys are so *much less fit* than he!'[2]

Someone sent him the July number of *To-Day*, containing an article about Sassoon by S.P.B. Mais and a photograph of the Glyn Philpot portrait (see above, p.37). 'It is just as well', Mais said,

> that when future generations find themselves forgetting, amid the calm, slack waters of peace, the horrors that belong to war, they should have the testimony and warning before them of someone who knew, having seen and felt and suffered, and in his suffering, told what he endured in no uncertain voice . . . Even now, above the tumult and the din of battle, his voice rings out, irrepressible, strangely elated and clear. . .

Owen tore the picture out and fixed it with some difficulty to his iron wall. It was in this shelter that Foulkes quoted some lines from Keats, and Owen's face lit up; 'from that time', Foulkes wrote later, 'I fancied he regarded me with real affection'.

Sassoonish attitudes to the war seemed to be spreading in the ranks, so much so that every platoon officer in the Fourth Army had to

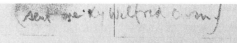

SPECIAL ORDER OF THE DAY
BY
GENERAL SIR H. S. RAWLINSON, BART.,
G.C.V.O., K.C.B., K.C.M.G.,
COMMANDING FOURTH ARMY.

There are indications that the enemies' "peace offensive" is creating the danger which is its object, namely, to divert the attention of officers and men from their single task of defeating the enemy.

All ranks are warned against the disturbing influence of dangerous peace talk.

The Field-Marshal Commanding-in-Chief wishes it to be understood clearly that at no time has there been a greater need of relentless effort or a fairer promise of great results, and orders the Army to concentrate its entire energy on bringing the operations in the field to a successful and decisive issue.

Peace talk in any form is to cease in the Fourth Army and Commanders of all Formations and Units will take immediate steps to ensure that this order is obeyed both in the spirit and in the letter.

HEADQUARTERS, FOURTH ARMY,
7th October, 1918.

Commanding Fourth Army.

PRINTED IN FRANCE BY ARMY PRINTING AND STATIONERY SERVICES.   PRESS A- 1918

Owen had to read this General Order to D Company on 10 October. He sent a copy to Sassoon.

promulgate an order from the GOC forbidding 'peace talk'. A senior lieutenant came back from leave in London, 'utterly disgusted with England's indifference to the real meaning of the war as we understand it'. Quoting Sassoon, Owen defined 'we' as 'every officer & man left, of the legions who have suffered and are dust'. The lieutenant's return ended Owen's brief captaincy. He became second in command again and moved from the uncomfortable tamboo to a worse tent. Several other officers returned from leave, including a Second Lieutenant James Kirk. The weather began to be wintry.

The battalion heard news of peace moves and spent a merry night ('I even discovered I could sing'). At home, however, Bottomley was still campaigning for total victory.

> No compromise, no negotiation, no forgiving – ruthless, relentless war to the knife, till the enemy lies prostrate, bleeding and beaten. That is what our sons and our brothers have died for; that is what, from regions we cannot penetrate, they are watching and waiting for us to do. Shall we betray them? God forbid![3]

'I am not depressed even by Bottomley's "NO! NO! NO!"', Owen said, adding hopefully that the whole Army had turned against *John Bull* at last.

From a subaltern's perspective there seemed no need to carry on. The Hindenburg Line had finally been cleared on 5 October, the French were back in St Quentin, and all along the Western Front the enemy was in retreat. Politicians saw things differently. The Germans still appeared capable of fierce resistance and they had become masters of the art of defence. If the pressure slackened, they might yet manage to dig in before a satisfactory armistice could be signed. Some people argued later that the war should have continued until Germany knew beyond doubt that she had been defeated by military victory, not by treachery or blockade. Others said the war's last casualties were the least necessary.

The last advance

On 18 October the brigade was suddenly on the move again, marching some twelve miles back to the Hindenburg Line at Lehaucourt, through Poeuilly, Vermand, Vadencourt, and Bellenglise. There was no longer any risk of shelling and the men were allowed to wear caps instead of helmets. They spent the night in the fortifications, Owen occupying a

Bohain on 10 October 1918, the day after liberation: local people and a Tommy posing by one of the mine craters. The flag had been kept hidden throughout the war.

dug-out with a tunnel fifty feet below the floor. He wrote home, saying that news of peace moves 'makes us feel that the Rumble on the horizon may cease any hour. I'm listening now, but it still goes on, a gigantic carpet-beating.'

At 8.45 a.m. on 20 October, the Manchesters started yet another day of footslogging. Some of the men were already exhausted. Owen 'had the painful duty of collecting & goading along the stragglers'. Presumably he was one of the officers in charge of the stragglers' party mentioned in brigade orders: it marched at the rear, at the pace of the slowest, and a horse-drawn ambulance followed. The march took seven hours, he said, and there was no food on the way. The place names were familiar from recent newspapers: Levergies, Sequehart, Fontaine-Uterte, Fresnoy-le-Grand, Bohain.

At Bohain the battalion reached 'the vestiges of civilization again'. The town was still inhabited; it had been one of the first to be captured intact, apart from damage caused by British shells and some huge mine craters, blown in the approach roads by the retreating Germans. Owen's fluent French came in useful for questioning civilians. The

A 'wretched, dirty, crawling community': two inhabitants of Busigny on 14 October.

Manchesters rested their feet for a while, then moved on to Busigny, where eighty-five reinforcements arrived on the 22nd. The newly-liberated villagers seemed 'a wretched, dirty, crawling community, afraid of *us*, some of them and no wonder after the shelling we gave them'. All the same, Owen was billeted in a cottage and treated kindly. During the next few days fatigue parties cleared roads, officers reconnoitred the route ahead, the men were paid, and the divisional general distributed medals and inspected the new arrivals.[4]

Mrs Owen wrote that she was ill in bed and too weak to get up. Her son told her to surround herself with the treasures he had bought in Scarborough and dream of walking with him to Haughmond. The battalion was not going into action, he said. Even though she was reading Tolstoy and finding courage to speak out against the war, it was best not to say too much, 'Lest aught she be disturbed, or grieved at all'.

On the 25th he at last overcame his reluctance to write to Gunston, who had managed to get a poem into *The Nation*. It was not a very good poem, but it had a faint trace of Owen's elegies and he assumed it was about the war dead (actually it had been inspired by a civilian cemetery which Gunston saw regularly from the train). It was enough to make a letter possible, although Gunston's conscience could not be allowed to escape.

You must not imagine when you hear we are 'resting' that we lie in bed smoking. We work or are on duty *always*. And last night my dreams were troubled by fairly close shelling. I believe only civilians in the village were killed (Thank God). In this house where I stay five healthy girls died of fright when *our* guns shelled the place last fortnight. You & I have always been open with each other: and therefore I must say that I feel sorry that you are neither in the flesh with Us nor in the spirit against war. You know why I could find no word of greeting for Gordon (on the occasion of his marriage.)[5]

He added he had seen no evidence of the German atrocities reported in the press (there had in fact been some, as in any war).

Gunston had met a new girl. Owen told him that he was himself being singled out by French girls for kisses and conversation, thanks to his French, so much so that the other officers had held a mock court martial on him. 'The dramatic irony was too killing, considering certain other things, not possible to tell in a letter.' Gunston could guess what that meant. War had not entirely destroyed the old trust between the cousins.

Owen was still reading Swinburne, the 'old song' which he and Gunston had revelled in at Dunsden.

> Now, ballad, gather poppies in thine hands
> And sheaves of brier and many rusted sheaves
> Rain-rotten in rank lands,
> Waste marigold and late unhappy leaves
> And grass that fades ere any of it be mown;
> And when thy bosom is filled full thereof
> Seek out Death's face ere the light altereth,
> And say 'My master that was thrall to Love
> Is become thrall to Death.'

The plan

The Germans had reached another canal and were preparing to make a stand. The Manchesters marched to St Souplet on 29 October. Next day

A railway bridge near Busigny, blown up by the retreating Germans.

the officers reconnoitred and in the afternoon led the troops by a cross-country route towards the front. The battalion marched in battle order, with D Company in support. This time a meal-break had been arranged for an hour just west of Bazuel, where the brigade was setting up its headquarters. Owen found a draughty tamboo and shared some chocolate from a Shrewsbury parcel with his new servant. The advance continued in the dark, reaching the line in an area of felled woodland in front of Pommereuil. The Germans had taken the timber, but the ground was boggy and tangled with undergrowth. Owen's platoon took over the defence of an isolated building marked on the maps as 'Forester's House', about a mile north-west of the Oise-Sambre canal. Things were fairly quiet, apart from shelling. The Army had not been in this territory since the retreat from Mons in 1914.

The gunners, sappers, and infantrymen who conferred over maps and aerial photographs in the next few days were faced with numerous difficulties. The canal was about forty feet across at water level, with wide tree-lined banks raised some four feet above the fields and separated from them by drainage ditches which the Germans had flooded. Observation was hampered by mist and hedges, in a countryside that was more like England than the wide uplands of the Somme. The brigade was responsible for a sector of the canal south of Landrecies and north of the village of Ors. The west bank was still in enemy hands. Beyond the east bank, protected by an elbow in the canal, the Germans were strongly positioned on rising ground at de la Motte Farm, having had time to dig in.

The 15th Lancashire Fusiliers had to fight hard for several days to clear the Happegarbes spur on the left, winning a VC and suffering heavy casualties from gas and shelling. When they took the spur, they found it impossible to hold, so its final capture was left until the main attack, when the enemy would be preoccupied with trying to prevent the brigade's other two battalions from crossing the canal. The 16th Lancashires in the centre were able to reach the railway, close to the canal. The 2nd Manchesters faced less opposition still, only some alarm posts which were not meant to be defended. In effect the ground just north of Ors, between the Forester's House and the waterway, was No Man's Land, and the battalion dealt with it as in the days of trench warfare, establishing ascendancy by means of night patrols.

218 Field Company, Royal Engineers, would have to build a bridge for each of the two battalions that were to cross. Amiens was now nearly ninety miles away by road, and the lines of supply and communication across the devastated areas were being badly disrupted by delayed action mines and other hazards. Some of the construction materials which were assembled along the canal for the Fourth Army were scavenged from dumps left by the Germans, but some had to be brought up by drivers and horses struggling for days over broken, congested roads. Wherever possible, temporary bridges were dismantled in the rear and brought forward for re-use; a depot was established at Bohain. During the week before the assault, the sappers reconnoitred the canal at the many planned crossing points and prepared a variety of bridges, each ingeniously adapted to its site.

The two bridges made for the 96th Brigade are described in the records as being of cork, timber, and wire. They probably conformed to a standard pattern: a narrow duckboard, supported by pairs of floats in simple timber frames. The floats were bales of cork slabs, tightly bound in wire netting; unlike barrels and petrol tins, these had been found to be almost impervious to bullets and shrapnel. Each pair was pre-assembled as a 'pier', weighing over 260 pounds; some four or five piers would have been needed for each bridge. The slatted duckboard was made in

The site of the attempted crossing, looking north from the west bank.

sections and fitted underneath with chocks and hooks, so that each section linked two piers, holding them in place. A 'spider' of steel cables, two from each float, would anchor the bridge to the bank, and poles would be lashed – with wire, because rope was too vulnerable to shrapnel – between the piers to give rigidity.

At the moment of the attack, 42 engineers and a company from 16th Highland Light Infantry, a pioneer battalion, were to carry the piers forward from their hiding place, drop them into the water one by one, fit the sections of duckboard and a rope handrail, and attach the poles and cables. The infantry would then be able to cross in single file. All this would take time, so 218 Field Company also made rafts, to be worked by paddles and towlines, for rapid advance crossings. (Such rafts were usually wooden crates, supported by bundles of reeds and wrapped in waterproof sheets; each carried, and could be carried by, four men.)[6]

If the canal was unpleasantly wide for the sappers, it was dangerously narrow for the gunners, who usually reckoned on an eighty-yard safety margin as a precaution against shells dropping short. Men and materials would have to be held back during the opening barrage. Too

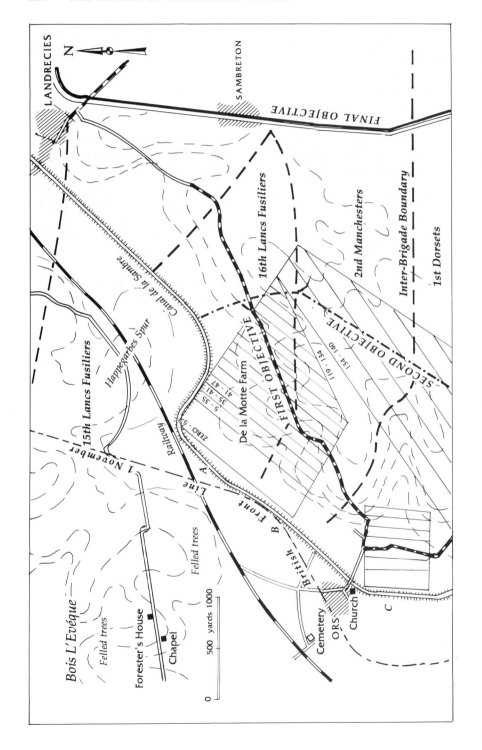

Where 96th Brigade should have crossed: the canal north of Ors, photographed by the RAF on 28 October 1918 (the railway runs across the top left
corner, and the village centre is just off the picture, bottom left). The Germans
still have forces on the west bank: the footbridge, which they will soon
demolish, is at approximately the site of the Manchesters' attempted crossing a
week later. Shell craters can be seen among the fields and orchards.

The Oise-Sambre canal between Landrecies and Ors, based on the plans drawn
up for 32nd Division in late October 1918. Crossing points in the assault were
to be at A (16th Lancashire Fusiliers), B (2nd Manchesters), C (1st Dorsets).
The start line of the barrage is shown on the east bank of the canal, to fall there
for 5 minutes from zero hour (5.45 a.m.). The barrage was then to lift 300
yards and remain stationary for 30 minutes, before creeping forward at the
rate of 100 yards every 6 minutes. It was an axiom that the success of an attack
depended on the infantry keeping as close behind the barrage as possible.
When the troops reached their first objective, the lane from Ors to Landrecies,
the barrage was to remain stationary for 15 minutes to allow them to catch up
and regroup if necessary.

The 'Maison Forestière de l'Ermitage' today. A ventilator to the brick-vaulted cellar can be seen on the right.

few shells might fail to eliminate the enemy from the east bank; too many might break it down. The Army had dreadful memories of what had happened to the dykes in Flanders in 1917. Already the low-lying fields on the far side were partly under water.

Observation may have suggested that the east bank itself was not strongly held. The commanders decided that the barrage should fall on it for only five minutes, then lift forward 300 yards to the higher ground in front of the farm and remain stationary for half an hour, preventing the enemy from sending reinforcements. In that time the bridges would be built. Once the two battalions had crossed, they would follow close behind the curtain of fire, which would start to creep forward at the rate of 100 yards every six minutes. The distance and timing of the first lift must have been a calculated gamble. In a normal attack on the Western Front, the opening barrage would have lasted longer and moved less far forward in its first advance.

At 6.15 on the evening of Thursday 31 October, Owen wrote home for what was to be the last time. Crammed into the 'Smoky Cellar of the Forester's House' with his platoon, he described the laughing men

Ors Church today, seen from the canal bank.

around him as they peeled potatoes and fed the fire with damp wood. They seemed a band of brothers, modern successors of Henry V's soldiers before Agincourt.

> It is a great life. I am more oblivious than alas! yourself, dear Mother, of the ghastly glimmering of the guns outside, & the hollow crashing of the shells.
>
> There is no danger down here, or if any, it will be well over before you read these lines.
>
> I hope you are as warm as I am; as serene in your room as I am here; and that you think of me never in bed as resignedly as I think of you always in bed. Of this I am certain you could not be visited by a band of friends half so fine as surround me here.

That was written for his mother's comfort. It is unlikely to be a complete statement of his feelings.

The battalion could do little but send out patrols and observers, keeping out of sight as much as possible. The enemy posts were cleared, the last of them being rushed by a fighting patrol and 'exterminated' on the Saturday evening. Everyone was briefed again and again, the newcomers being given special instruction in the use of flares for the

The canal south of Ors, soon after 4 November.

information of aircraft, a new method of communication which Colonel Mitchell in Scarborough had probably never heard of. Pairs of men were detailed to make light bridges for crossing the flooded ditches. Others were to carry the rafts. Dress was to be full battle order, with steel helmet, leather jerkin, waterproof sheet, a day's rations, filled water bottle, and 170 rounds of ammunition. Stress was laid on the need for silence and concealment. Officers were told that although counter-attacks were more than likely there could be no question of withdrawal. Paths to the canal were taped out and planks laid over waterlogged ground. Meticulous preparations of this kind had been typical of trench warfare; they were not so appropriate for an unpredictable fight in which speed, secrecy, and initiative were going to be crucial. The Germans watched and waited.

The outcome

In the dark before dawn on Monday 4 November the brigade quietly took up positions. To the north the 15th Lancashires still had to take the last of the high ground. On their right the 16th were drawn up in an orchard, where they lay down and waited for zero hour. The Manchesters were still on the southernmost flank (the inter-brigade boundary lay immediately to their right, just north of Ors). They assembled along a lane about a quarter of a mile back from the canal, with D Company once again one of the two in the lead.

The guns opened up at 5.45 a.m., punctual as ever, and for five minutes the east bank erupted in flame and protective smoke. As soon as the barrage lifted, the leading companies dashed forward, bridging the ditches and lining the west bank to give covering fire. The sappers and pioneers brought up the heavy piers and began pushing them out across the water. Writing his report later, the CO of the Manchesters was understandably anxious to stress how efficient it had all been. But from the German side came what he described as 'the most terrific Machine Gun fire, heavy Trench Mortar fire, and spasmodic Artillery fire'. The gamble had failed. Three hundred yards away the barrage drummed steadily on the empty fields.

'There is to be no retirement under any circumstances': orders were specific on this point. The engineers worked feverishly. Gas mingled with the thick mist and smoke. Bullets thudded into the timbers as men handled them, striking sparks from the wire. It seemed impossible that anyone could survive, let alone reach the far bank. Casualties became so numerous that the bridging effort weakened. Seeing the need for stronger cover, James Kirk mounted a Lewis gun on a raft and paddled out until he could shoot at ten yards range. When he ran out of ammunition, more was sent over to him. He was hit in the face and arm, but kept firing. Under this protection, a sapper named Archibald went out on the bridge to finish it; other men joined him, encouraged by his example, but all were soon hit or gassed. The RE commander, Major Waters, realized he had no officers left, so he coolly walked over himself to complete the fastenings. He came back and led two platoons of Manchesters across. Kirk was hit for the third time and killed. Then a shell smashed the bridge.

There is no eye-witness account of Owen's death. When the bridge

Above left: The temporary wooden cross on Owen's grave.

Above right: The permanent headstone in Ors cemetery.

Left: The British stones (Owen's is third from left, back row) and 'Cross of Sacrifice', seen from among the village graves. Ors church is in the background.

was wrecked, the Manchesters tried repeatedly but in vain to repair it, and then took to the rafts. Two survivors described to Mrs Owen later how he had patted them and said 'Well done' and 'You are doing well my boy', as they struggled with equipment on the bank. Foulkes did not see what happened, having become a casualty himself, but several people told him afterwards that Owen had boarded a raft and been hit while out on the water.[7]

At about 7 a.m. the operation was called off, and Divisional Headquarters were asked for further orders. The CO's report emphasizes the methodical discipline of the withdrawal, which was made in stages from about 8.30 a.m. under cover of the bank. Double runners were sent north and south, soon reporting back that the 1st Dorsets had

2nd Lieut. W. E. S. Owen, M.C.
Manchester Regt. He was the eldest
son of Mr. and Mrs. T. Owen, and
was killed in action near the Sambre
Canal on November 4, 1918

One of the many photographs of dead officers published in 1914–19 (*The Sphere*, 29 March 1919).

found a weak spot in the enemy defences just below Ors church; the engineers had succeeded in building several bridges there. The Manchester support and reserve companies were sent down to cross, and the two lead companies followed.

The 16th Lancashires had fared no better. They were under the command of Marshall, the 'Terrible Major' (now Acting Lieutenant-Colonel), who led them 'without any regard to his own safety', until he was killed leading a vain attempt to get across their damaged bridge. The survivors turned south to join the Manchesters. These two failures were almost the only ones suffered that day in what was the Fourth Army's last concerted attack. Victoria Crosses were later awarded to Kirk, Archibald, Waters, and Marshall.

The 96th Brigade soon rejoined the advance. The 15th Lancashires had cleared the spur and reached the canal bank; they later crossed at Landrecies. The Germans at de la Motte Farm put up a ferocious

The Lord Lieutenant of Berkshire unveiling the Reading war memorial on 27 July 1932. Behind him stands the memorial's honorary architect, Leslie Gunston, ARIBA.

resistance until they became isolated. The 2nd Manchesters reached their first objective by noon and the final line next morning. Their casualties had been 2 officers killed and 3 wounded, 22 other ranks killed, 81 wounded, and 18 missing. By 6 November the battalion was 'comfortably billeted' at Sambreton. Three months later it was in Bonn.

Owen was buried with the other dead in a corner of the cemetery at Ors, a green and peaceful place above the village. The grave was marked with a temporary wooden cross, recording him as still a second lieutenant. On 5 November the *London Gazette* announced his promotion to full lieutenant, backdated to 4 December 1917. On the 8th the award of his MC was recorded in the battalion diary. The permanent gravestone bears his final rank and a misquotation from his sonnet, 'The End', supplied by Mrs Owen: 'Shall life renew these bodies? Of a truth all death will he annul'. In the poem the second sentence is also a question.

In 1991 the Western Front Association set up a memorial to all those who had died on the canal. The local gendarme, who is a builder in his spare time, laid the bricks in English bond and gave his services for nothing. The unveiling took place on 29 September. A village band played 'The roses of Picardy', and the Chairman of the Wilfred Owen Association made a speech in French. The Mayor of Ors expressed pride that the village was the last resting place of a famous English poet, '*mort au champ d'honneur*'. The plaque includes a quotation from Owen's 'With an Identity Disc'. That sonnet, like 'The End', was written before he met Sassoon. The poems of his last year do not lend themselves to memorial inscriptions.

APPENDIX

THE POEMS OF THE LAST YEAR: AN APPROXIMATE CHRONOLOGY

Abbreviations

CPF *Wilfred Owen: The Complete Poems and Fragments* (1983)
  CL *Wilfred Owen: The Collected Letters* (1967)
   F Fragment
 PP *Pompeiian Parchment* (watermark)
 SB *Society Bond* (watermark)
   * Owen used the same type of paper for at least one draft of each of these poems.
   # At least one draft of each of these poems is on *Hieratica Bond* paper (large size), also used for late November – early December letters.
   § Owen used the same type of paper for drafts of these poems, and for his Preface and its list of contents.

The list below includes all Owen's war poems and fragments, and all other verse begun after his arrival at Craiglockhart, arranged in possible order of first composition. It has to be partly guesswork. No one can know for sure when most of his poems were started. In many cases the only clue is the type of paper used for such drafts as happen to survive; usually that does no more than suggest when the poem may have been in progress.

War poems before Craiglockhart

Almost all Owen's poems which refer specifically to war seem to have been started after he met Sassoon in mid-August 1917. The few exceptions, all expressing fairly conventional attitudes, are: '1914' (sonnet, dated 1914), 'An Imperial Elegy' (F, ?1916), 'It was a navy boy' (ballad, ?1915), 'A New Heaven' (sonnet, dated 1916), 'With an Identity Disc' (sonnet, spring 1917). A 1915 fragment for what seems to have been planned as a long poem on 'Perseus' includes a description of the German 'Beast' (*CPF*, 449).

'The Ballad of Peace and War' or 'The Ballad of Purchase Moneys' was first drafted no later than July 1915. It was subsequently revised as 'Ballad of Kings and Christs' and again, perhaps in winter 1917–18, as 'The Women and the Slain'. The revisions were just enough to make 'The Women and the Slain' a contradiction of the soldiers-as-Arthurs-and-Christs theme of the original version.

'Sonnet/On Seeing a Piece of Our Heavy Artillery . . .' survives only as a ?Ripon draft, but Sassoon would not have allowed that 'Our' in the title, nor the poem's anti-German implications. The first draft could well have been written in France early in 1917 (*CPF* suggests July 1917).

Craiglockhart before Sassoon
(late June to mid-August 1917)

('The Ballad of Lady Yolande': *CPF* says 'late June-July', but one page is
    dated 8 June, before Owen left France. Continued at Craiglockhart.)
'The Fates': 31 June-2 July (*CL*, 474).
*'The Wrestlers' (Antaeus): July, redrafted early in 1918 for *The Hydra*
    and possibly published there in February (no copy survives of this
    number).
'Sweet is your antique body': a summer poem to Arthur Newboult,
    perhaps written soon after Owen met him in July. (*CPF*'s 'Craiglock-
    hart, probably . . . December' must be a mistake.)
*'Song of Songs': 'done here' (Craiglockhart), apparently before Sassoon
(*CL*, 487).
'Lines to a Beauty seen in Limehouse' (F): on *Imperial Fine* paper, used
    for July/mid-August letters.
*'Has your soul sipped': earlier of two drafts on *Imperial Fine*.

Craiglockhart after Sassoon
(mid-August to late October 1917)

*'The Dead-Beat': 21 August (*CL*, 485). Later rewritten.

*'My Shy Hand': 29–30 August (MS dated) .

*'I know the music' (F). *'But I was looking' (F).

*'Anthem for Doomed Youth': mentioned on 25 September (*CL*, 496).

*'Six o'clock in Princes' Street'. *'S.I.W.' *'The Chances'. *'Beauty' (F).

*'The Sentry': the first rough sketch is on the same sheet as material used in 'Six o'clock'. The final version is September 1918.

*'Inspection': *CPF*'s precise 'Drafted . . . in August . . . completed in September' seems unjustified.

*'The Next War': in *The Hydra*, 29 September.

*'Dulce et Decorum Est': draft dated 8 October.

*'Disabled': shown to Graves by Sassoon, 13 October.

*'Winter Song': an autumn poem to Arthur Newboult. Draft dated 18 October.

'The Promisers': drafted on an Edinburgh cafe bill.

'The Letter': the only MS, a fair copy, is on *SB* (see below), but the Sassoonish style may suggest a Craiglockhart origin.

#'Conscious': again, the MSS, all fair copies, are later, but the style may suggest Craiglockhart.

'At a Calvary near the Ancre': the only MS is an undated copy by Susan Owen.

'The Ballad of Many Thorns': *CPF*, 122. Draft on *PP*.

'From My Diary, July 1914': perhaps written in response to Sassoon's praise of 'Song of Songs', which is similar in style. The only MS is on *PP*.

'Soldier's Dream': late October (*CL*, 512). Draft on *PP*.

1917 after Craiglockhart

*'Asleep': MS dated 14 November.

#'Earth's wheels': apparently sent to Sassoon in November.

#'Apologia pro Poemate Meo': latest draft dated November.

'I saw his round mouth's crimson' (F?): on a type of paper used for drafting 'Apologia'.

'Spells and Incantation': drafts on Regent Palace Hotel and *Ivy* paper.

#'Wild with all Regrets': 'begun and ended two days ago' (6 December).

MS dated 5 December. Revised at Ripon as 'A Terre'.

#'Cramped in that funnelled hole': usually treated as F, but probably more correctly regarded as draft work for 'Exposure'.

#'Hospital Barge': MS dated 8 December.

#'Le Christianisme'.

#'The Show'.

'Mourn for the nights to come' (F): no evidence for date, except that it seems to anticipate 'Mental Cases'. (*CPF* suggests November-December.)

Early 1918 (January to early March)

'Miners': 13 or 14 January, inspired by newspaper reports.

'With those that are become' (F): quotes from Wilde and anticipates 'Strange Meeting'. (*CPF* suggests London/late 1917.)

'Reunion': two surviving drafts, one impossible to date, the other on *Ivy* paper (other *Ivy* MSS are November-March). (*CPF*'s June-July 1917 date seems unfounded.)

'Page Eglantine', 'The Rime of the Youthful Mariner', 'Who is the god of Canongate': ballads on Clarence Gardens paper.

'I am the ghost of Shadwell stair': one draft on *SB*.

'The Last Laugh': in draft as 'Last Words' by 18 February (*CL*, 534). Another draft, on *SB*, dated 5 March.

Ripon (12 March to 5 June 1918)

'As bronze may be much beautified' (F): first attempt, dated Good Friday (29 March), on the back of an old sonnet.

'Greater Love': first drafted on the backs of old sonnets.

'A Tear Song': drafts on *PP* and *SB*.

'Insensibility': drafts on *PP* and *SB*. (*CPF* suggests a Craiglockhart start; the style seems markedly later. See note on *PP* below.)

'Strange Meeting': drafts on *PP*(?) and *SB*.

'Schoolmistress': the only draft is on *SB*.

'Exposure': earliest draft work probably December 1917. Complete draft on *SB*. In both lists of contents. Last draft may be September.

§'Ode for a Poet': Owen added a second section in September and changed the title to 'Elegy in April and September'. Paper types seem to confirm that the poem was composed in those months.

'The Send-Off': in progress, April-early May (*CL*, 550).

'Arms and the Boy': fair copy dated 3 May.

'Mental Cases': mentioned in May letters.

'The Parable of the Old Man and the Young': appears in both lists of contents, so no later than early June.

List of contents for 'Disabled and Other Poems': on *SB*.

§Preface and §list of contents: probably late Ripon.

§'Futility': in *The Nation*, 15 June.

§'The Calls': *CPF* says 'Scarborough . . . May', but Owen was at Ripon then.

§'O true to the old equities' (F): on verso of, but maybe later than, 'The Calls'.

Scarborough (June to August 1918)

'Training': MS dated June 1918.

'The roads also' (F): influenced by the Sitwells, whose work Owen did not know until after 15 June (*CL*, 559).

'The Kind Ghosts': the only draft, a fair copy, is dated 30 July.

'Spring Offensive': title appears in a short list, ?August. On 22 September Owen sent the first 17 lines to Sassoon, asking 'Is this worth going on with?'

France (September to October 1918)

'Smile, Smile, Smile': draws on a 19 September newspaper report. Final draft dated 23 September.

The evidence of watermarks

Where a watermark or recognizable type of paper occurs in Owen's letters before 1917, it does so for one limited period only, so a poem on similar paper is likely to belong to the same period. This rule breaks down in 1917–18, when he often had to work in a hurry. The dates given in *CPF* (and in the abridged paperback edition) are sometimes more definite than the evidence warrants. When *CPF* says a poem was 'written' in a particular period, it often does so on the basis of watermarks alone. Two key 1917–18 watermarks are *PP* and *SB*.

The date of PP. Owen used this good-quality paper for three letters between 5 November 1917 (his first letter to Sassoon) and 24 January 1918, and for drafts of at least twenty-six poems. One of these poems is 'Soldier's Dream', 'the last piece from Craiglockhart' (i.e. late October). *CPF* assumes – as I used to – that any *PP* MS is likely to belong to that October-January period, even though twenty of these MSS are fair copies of sonnets, all first composed before 1917. *CPF* arranges poems in supposed order of 'final' (i.e. last surviving) drafts and thus has to print these sonnets among the 1917–18 war poems, where they are jarringly out of place. Another difficulty is that several of the war poems drafted on *PP* seem unlikely to have been started as early as October-January.

One fact may give the solution: Owen was at home, for the first time in 1917, when he wrote his letter to Sassoon. He may well have had a stock of *PP* in his desk, having bought it in 1916 for the sonnets (he was thinking of publishing a little book of them then). Naturally he used his best paper for Sassoon. He used more of it for redrafting 'Soldier's Dream' and other poems he had begun at Craiglockhart. He took the old sonnets with him to Scarborough and Ripon, where he used the backs of several for new work at Easter.

There seem to have been some blank sheets left. 'Insensibility', probably 'Strange Meeting', and 'A Tear Song' exist in two drafts, the earlier on *PP* and the later on *SB*. (I guess the first 'Strange Meeting' draft is on *PP*; the measurements given in *CPF* almost correspond, but the MS was framed by C. Day Lewis, leaving the watermark invisible.) The three poems are thus likely to be contemporary; the style and content of the first two suggest Ripon. (Simon Wormleighton, 'Wilfred Owen and A.C. Benson', *Notes & Queries*, December 1990, 435–37, notices an echo in 'Insensibility' of Benson's *Where No Fear Was*, which Owen was reading at Ripon in May.)

In my opinion, therefore, the October 1917-January 1918 date for *PP* is too narrow. Owen may have used this paper in 1916 and at any time from November 1917 until at least June 1918.

The date of SB. Used for four letters, January-February 1918, and drafts of eleven poems. *CPF* uses this evidence inconsistently, limiting some of the drafts to January-February, some (including 'Strange Meeting') to January-March, and one ('Insensibility') to January. *CPF* also overlooks one more *SB* MS, a crucial one: the list of contents for 'Disabled and Other Poems', which includes the titles of all the poems known to have been composed at Ripon. So the *SB* period must be at least January-*early June*, to include the whole of Owen's time at Ripon.

SOURCES AND NOTES

Abbreviations

EB   *The Poems of Wilfred Owen*, ed. Edmund Blunden (1931)
CL   *Wilfred Owen: Collected Letters*, ed. Harold Owen and John Bell (1967)
CPF   *Wilfred Owen: The Complete Poems and Fragments*, ed. Jon Stallworthy, 2 vols (1983)
JS   Jon Stallworthy, *Wilfred Owen: A Biography* (1974)
OEF   Owen Collection, English Faculty Library, Oxford
OTP   Dominic Hibberd, *Owen the Poet* (1986)

Principal sources

(a) Letters.
Quotations from Owen's letters are from *CL*, with some additions and amendments from MSS. The editors of *CL* did not see the original MS letters to Leslie Gunston, but were supplied with typed copies; I have quoted some material omitted from those copies, and some other passages omitted by *CL*. Many of the dates given to letters in *CL* seem to have been copied from postmarks by Harold Owen when he threw away the hundreds of envelopes; I have silently amended these dates when Owen probably posted a letter a day or two after writing it (e.g., a letter which he marked 'Friday' and which his brother dated '13 August' I assume to have been written on Friday 10 August 1917, not on Monday 13th). The original letters are at the University of Texas at Austin, except those to Gunston (OEF) and Sassoon (Columbia University).

(b) Poems.
Quotations from Owen's poems are from *CPF*. The principal verse MSS are in the British Library; OEF has many folios of draft work and a few fair copies.

(c) Miscellaneous MSS.
Owen's other papers (essays, notes, letters to him, etc.) are in OEF, as are his books and many family items.

(d) Memoirs by people who knew Owen.
H.R. Bate, 'Sixty Years After', unpublished autobiography, Imperial War Museum; 'Sixty Years Ago', *Blackwood's Magazine* (November 1975).
John Foulkes, four pages of unsigned notes written for Edmund Blunden, c. 1930 (University of Texas), partly quoted in *EB*.
Robert Graves, *Goodbye to All That* (1929 and later editions); *In Broken Images: Selected Letters 1914–1946*, ed. Paul O'Prey (1982).
Conal O'Riordan, 'One More Fortunate', *Martial Medley* (1931), 357–61; 'The Poets Are Cheerful!', *John O'London's Weekly* (6 June 1941), 225–26.
Harold Owen, *Journey from Obscurity*, 3 vols (1963–65).
Siegfried Sassoon, *Diaries 1915–1918* (1983), *Diaries 1920–1922* (1981), *Diaries 1923–1925* (1985), ed. Rupert Hart-Davis; *Siegfried's Journey* (1945).
C.K. Scott Moncrieff, letter, *New Witness* (2 January 1920), 117; 'The Poets there are. III – Wilfred Owen', *New Witness* (10 December 1920), 574–75; 'Wilfred Owen', letter, *Nation and Athenaeum* (26 March 1921), 909–10.
Osbert Sitwell, *Noble Essences* (1950).
Others. Mary Gray and others are quoted in *EB*, Arthur and Mary Newboult in *CL*. OEF, and the Owen and Blunden collections at Texas, have letters from several people who knew Owen; Columbia University has letters from Susan and Harold Owen to Sassoon.

(e) Military history.
In Chapters 6–7 I have taken many details from the War Diaries kept by 32nd Division, 96th Brigade, and the brigade's various units (Public Record Office WO 95.2396, etc.). The files contain numerous orders and reports. Published sources include: *History of the Great War / Military Operations / France and Belgium 1918*, ed. J.E. Edmonds, vol. 5 (1947); A. Montgomery, *The Story of the Fourth Army in the Battles of the Hundred Days* (1920); R.E. Priestley, *Breaking the Hindenburg Line* (1919); H.C. Wylly, *History of the Manchester Regiment*, vol.2 (1925). Montgomery's maps show the movements of each brigade on the Hindenburg Line and of each battalion at Ors.

(f) Other.
See *OTP* for detailed notes and bibliography.

Notes to the Chapters

Items in (d) above are referred to by surname and date only.

Introduction

1. Owen and some 1917–18 records spell the name incorrectly as 'Cérisy'. The site of the CCS is marked today by the Cerisy-Gailly cemetery, close to the canalised Somme.
2. The evidence is scanty. Graves (1982), 206–9, quotes a letter from Sassoon: Owen 'was not "in a very shaky condition", and said so little about being accused of "cold feet" that I always regarded it as a negligible affair'. Sassoon is protesting at the comments in Graves (1929), where Owen is said to have been 'accused of cowardice' by his CO. Sassoon's denial implies that there *was* an accusation. For further evidence, see *OTP*, 76–77.

Chapter 1: Return to England

1. Gordon Gunston was an optician. The Owens were perhaps always envious of the Gunstons. John Gunston, Owen's uncle, a prosperous pork butcher, had a country villa built for himself and his family in 1908, near Reading. Alpenrose had six bedrooms, and in the large grounds were a field with a cow or two, an orchard, a pig-sty, and a vegetable garden. The Owens' house in Shrewsbury was a modest semi, with a narrow strip of garden.

The hut at which Leslie was working was one of many provided at Army camps by the Young Men's Christian Association as havens where troops could relax, write letters, read, hear music, and obtain refreshments.

Chapter 2: Hospital

1. Information about Craiglockhart (now part of Napier Polytechnic)

from *The Hydra* (see *OTP*, 206); Napier archives; Sassoon, *Sherston's Progress* (1936) and *Diaries* (1983).

2. 'Extract from ye Chronicles of Sir Wilfred de Salope, Knight', *The Hydra* (15 September 1917).

3. For Brock, see *OTP*, 84–94, 195–96. His fullest account of his work in 1916–18 is in his 'The Re-Education of the Adult: The Neurasthenic in War and Peace', *Sociological Review*, x (Summer 1918), 25–40; I have taken details and phrases from this. Most descriptions of Owen at Craiglockhart concentrate on Sassoon's doctor, W.H.R. Rivers, but there is no evidence that Owen had any contact with him. The relationship between Rivers and Sassoon is the central theme of Pat Barker's interesting novel, *Regeneration* (1991), in which Owen and Brock make brief appearances.

4. The Camera Obscura predates Geddes and has outlasted his exhibitions; it can still be visited.

5. Simon Wormleighton points out that Brock (*Health and Conduct*, 1923, 171–72) is misquoting Tennyson's 'the spectres of the mind' (*In Memoriam*, xcvi). The poems about inner visions are 'Has your soul sipped' and 'Lines to a Beauty seen in Limehouse'. For Owen's pararhyme, see *OTP*.

6. Craiglockhart registers (PRO MH 106. 1887) record a Second Lieutenant Charles Mayes, RGA, aged 19, admitted 3 March, discharged 2 November.

7. Open Spaces Committee minute books (National Library of Scotland) in Brock's hand record a ceaseless battle against vandalism, theft, and weeds. There were eight or nine gardens by 1914; one is preserved in West Port as a memorial to Geddes.

8. 'News from the Front', *Cambridge Magazine* (2 June 1917), 679. Reprinted here for the first time.

9. Quoted from MS. Omitted from *CL*, 492, 494.

10. 'sugarless tea   enslavement': phrases from an outline for a satire on Edinburgh civilians (*CPF*, 256).

11. *OTP*, 120.

12. Aylmer Strong, *A Human Voice* (1917). Strong called on Sassoon in September; Owen may have met him. Sassoon gave the book to Owen, dating it 26 October. In *Siegfried's Journey* he records that the dinner at the Club was on 3 November and notes that Owen had exactly a year to live.

Chapter 3: Light Duties

1. Sassoon (1983), 196. For Ross and his friends, see Maureen Borland, *Wilde's Devoted Friend: A Life of Robert Ross* (1990); Sassoon (1945); Sitwell (1950); *OTP*, 196–97. For Burton, see Sassoon (1981, 1985).

2. See Owen's letter of 16 November, reproduced in this chapter. His mention of a 'key' is followed by a reference to Gunston's current girlfriend.

3. The term 'Camp Commandant' was a suggestion by John Bell, based on his own Army experience. Information about Mitchell from Bate.

4. The former Clarence Gardens (now Clifton) Hotel has only one tower, with a five-light window on each floor. I assume Owen's reference to his 'five-windowed turret' and his liking for high places means he was on the top floor.

5. *Theocritus, Bion and Moschus*, tr. Andrew Lang (1906). Owen's copy, bought in Scarborough in December, later belonged to Gunston, who gave it to me. It is now in OEF.

6. Quoted from MS. Omitted from *CL*, 516.

7. For the argument between Sassoon and Graves, see my '"The Patchwork Flag" (1918): an unrecorded book by Robert Graves', *Review of English Studies*, xli. 164 (1990), 521–32.

8. Sassoon (1985), 140.

9. Scott Moncrieff (December 1920).

10. Like Bate and Owen, Priestley trained with the Artists' Rifles. He was commissioned into the 7th Manchesters in December 1915 and promoted lieutenant in July 1917. He was on the permanent reserve by 1918, and his name disappears from the Army List by the autumn of that year.

11. For Bainbrigge, see Scott Moncrieff (December 1920); *CL*, 532, n. 1; T. d'Arch Smith, *Love in Earnest* (1970); Martin Taylor, ed., *Lads: Love Poetry of the Trenches* (1989). *CL* identifies Claus as Emile Claus, the distinguished Belgian painter, who was certainly in England during the war, but the Army List shows a Second Lieutenant W.M. Claus, 5th Manchesters, seconded to 1st (Res) Garrison Yorks LI.

12. *OTP*, 155.

13. 'Sonnets': Owen had his old sonnets with him a fortnight later and had presumably been considering them at Scarborough, perhaps

further evidence that life there had begun to distract him from war poetry.

Chapter 4: Training Again

1. Details from *A Ripon Record 1887–1986*, ed. Edna Ellis and others (Chichester, 1986). The military area was divided into North and South Camps. The Yorkshire Photographic Archive (University College of Ripon and York St John, Ripon) has a map of the South Camp which shows a cluster of huts numbered '32' on the north edge of the common; Owen's first letter from Ripon was from '32 Lines'. Some of his later letters were from the Officers' YMCA Hut in the North Camp, probably a daytime common room.

2. Owen said later that the letter contained 'wild statements' (*CL*, 547); the surviving fragment opens with a reference to 'your pleasaunce of Alpenrose'.

3. 'Borrage' is the correct spelling. *JS*, 259, implies that Owen took up residence in the cottage, but he seems to have had a regular walk between it and the dormitory hut. He would probably not have been able to live out of camp without revealing his whereabouts ('No one here knows of my retreat').

4. *CPF*'s October 1917-January 1918 date for the composition of 'Greater Love' is based on watermark evidence, but the watermark is irrelevant: Owen was not necessarily using newly-acquired paper (see Appendix). The 'As bronze' fragment is the clue to follow.

5. Harold Owen (1965), III, ch. 11.

6. When he heard Sassoon had destroyed some of Owen's letters, Harold Owen replied: 'Thank you for the burning. I too have done some of this here and there – I shall have more to do when I get deeper into the editing' (1 January 1957, Columbia University). See *OTP*, 199–201, and my 'Wilfred Owen's Letters', *The Library*, 4 (September 1982), 273–87.

7. Letters from Graves to Scott Moncrieff (National Library of Scotland, Acc 7243), October 1917–5 May 1918 (this last letter is from the School of Instruction). On 23 May Graves wrote to Sassoon from Wales: 'Scott Moncrieff is sending Wilfred Owen here, when he's a bit stronger, to my battalion' (Graves, 1982, 94). Owen's New Year remark about going back to be with the troops referred specifically to Etaples; he may

have been thinking of a staff job at base, not front line service.

8. Sonnet and letter in OEF. See *OTP*, 198–99.

9. Text from *Poetry of the Great War: An Anthology*, ed. Dominic Hibberd and John Onions (1986). Owen quoted the poem inaccurately after his own boat journey (*CL*, 570).

10. W.B. Yeats, 'On being asked for a war poem'. Yeats's views on Owen are well known.

11. The evidence seems persuasive that the Preface and its list are late Ripon. The other list seems slightly earlier; it may be the one Owen referred to on 29 May. The two lists prove that all his war poems were at least in draft by 5 June, except five known to be later (see Appendix). Provisional titles include 'Only fifty yards' and (?) 'The Light' for 'The Sentry', and 'To Any Woman' for 'Greater Love'. Titles not yet satisfactorily explained include 'Shell Shock Cases/Troops' (?'Mental Cases') and 'Consistency'. Either of these or 'Ode' could conceivably refer to 'Insensibility', the most puzzling omission (but 'Ode' is more probably 'Ode for a Poet'). The only other omissions are 'Disabled' (taken for granted as the title poem?), 'Earth's wheels' (superseded by 'Strange Meeting'), 'Schoolmistress', 'At a Calvary'.

Chapter 5: General Service

1. Owen refers to 'Camp', not 'barracks'. The tents were probably on the open land adjoining the barrack compound, an area used for territorial camps before the war.

2. The British mania for secrecy can have few greater monuments than the impenetrable Ministry archives. All I can discover from courteous officials is that Owen's file was probably 'weeded' out in the 1930s. Nevertheless, there is reason to believe that it still existed twenty years ago. My account of War Office decisions about Owen is based on Scott Moncrieff (1920–21) and scattered clues in *CL*.

3. The shortlist (*CPF*, 540) is on the same type of paper as four of the MSS sent to Osbert. His letter to Mrs Owen (OEF) is undated but seems to be c. December 1918. For Edith's editing, see her *Selected Letters* (1970). Most of the MSS which *CPF* notes as summer 1918 revisions were copies hastily made for *Wheels*; there was no time available for the sort of serious revising that Owen had been able to do at Ripon.

4. The Army List, November 1918, shows Owen as third senior out of

over eighty second lieutenants in the 5th Battalion; all those after him were commissioned in 1917–18. Even allowing for his six months in hospital, his progress seems to have been unusually slow.

5. 'Letter to S.S. from Bryn-y-Pin', published 1990 (see above, ch. 3, n. 7).

6. Sassoon (1983), 275. The distraught poem is in Sassoon, *The War Poems* (1983), 130.

7. Owen alludes to 'Testament' (see above, ch. 4, n. 9.).

8. Sassoon to Marsh, 'Thursday' [15 August 1918], (Berg Collection, NY). The Reform Club records show that Meiklejohn had two guests on the 15th, Owen and 'Captain ----on' (name illegible). I am grateful to the club librarian, Mr Simon Blundell, for this information; he tells me that Owen's name also appears as Ross's guest for lunch on 23 January and 17 May 1918.

9. Sitwell (1950), 108–9; Sassoon (1945), 71–72.

10. Sassoon (1945) comments that this was the only chance for 'intimate talk' between himself and Owen in 1918, so I assume that he made his stabbing threat on this occasion (*CL*, 571, n. 3).

11. The first medical was on Sunday 11 August. If medicals were usually on Sundays, Owen may have been passed fit on the 18th – hence the tone of his Monday letter, and perhaps the recurrence of his trench foot, a disorder which seems to have caused no trouble once he reached France. Or the second medical may have been on the 25th; the adjutant's order followed next day.

Chapter 6: Return to France

1. For Etaples and the mutiny, see Gloden Dallas and Douglas Gill, *The Unknown Army* (1985).

2. O'Riordan (1931, 1941). For McClymont, see *JS*, 270.

3. The lines are a rapid addition in pencil. If they were written in October, as is quite possible, they refer to immediate experience.

4. Sources are inconsistent on some details. I follow the majority of PRO papers in ascribing the attack on Joncourt to the Lancashires, although the Manchesters may have been in support. One source says all the tanks reached their objectives. Swiss Cottage was clearly one or more buildings, perhaps a farm, not a trench. MC citations for 1–2 October are in *The London Gazette* (30 July 1919): Owen (9761), Foulkes

(9733), and at least five others in the battalion (Lieutenants Cobley and Taylor, Second Lieutenants Burrows and Johnson, CSM Mutters). All these citations mention resisting heavy counter-attacks. Second Lieutenant Whitehead, 16th Lancashires, won an MC for his part in getting up the rations on the first night and leading a company in the line next day.

5. I assume Owen became OC D Company during the initial attack, because he refers to the seraph as a 'sergeant-major', a company rank.

Chapter 7: The Battle of the Sambre Canal

1. Simon Wormleighton points out the continuity in this 10 October letter: 'It was easy . . . to tell [O'Riordan] everything about oneself. / I have nothing to tell *you* except . . . ' (*CL*, 582, my italics). *JS*, 280, assumes Jones was killed, but Owen was responsible for casualty reports and described Jones on the 10th as 'happily wounded'. Philip Guest tells me a Private Thomas Jones, Manchester Regiment, died on 1 October, but the surname was a common one in the regiment.

2. Sentence omitted from *CL*, 586.

3. *John Bull* (14 September 1918). Owen may have found an old copy, but Bottomley made many similar pronouncements. (Bottomley was suggesting on 14 September that victory might come before Christmas, a novel idea at that stage; a month later Mary Owen thought the war might go on until mid-1919.)

4. Owen may have been given his MC on this occasion, although the award is not entered in the battalion diary until after his death. *CL*, 580, n. 2, says the award was 'immediate' (i.e. made on the field, 1–3 October), but this seems unlikely; Owen said on the 10th that he was glad he had been recommended '& hope I get it'.

5. Paragraph quoted from MS (*CL* text is defective). Gunston's poem was 'Les Morts', *The Nation* (5 October 1918), 18.

6. For plans of rafts and bridges, see the *Bridging* volume in *The Work of the Royal Engineers in the European War, 1914–19* (Chatham, 1921). *JS*, 285, describes the sappers dragging 'their serpentine bridge' down to the canal, but the size and weight of the structure would have made that a difficult operation; the piers must have been joined up on the water. In the standard pattern, each float measured about 4ft × 2ft × 1ft. To form a 'pier', two floats were set about 3ft apart, their longest axes parallel,

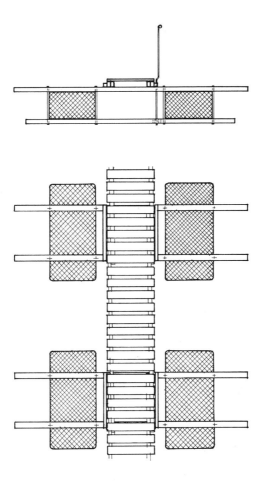

and compressed with long bolts between four 10ft spars. The projecting ends of the spars presumably served as carrying handles. 32nd Division's diary mentions men lashing poles to floats while under fire. The two bridges were put across in half an hour, a record time.

7. Susan Owen to Sassoon, 10 September [?1920] (Columbia University). *EB* quotes Foulkes except at this point, where Blunden reverts to the earlier information given to Mrs Owen and adds that Owen was killed on the bank; presumably he took this detail from Mrs Owen, but she does not mention it in her letter to Sassoon. Foulkes seems confident of the facts, and I prefer his version. Antaeus had to leave the ground.

ACKNOWLEDGEMENTS

FOR many years I had the friendship of the late Leslie Gunston; a few weeks before his death in 1988 he gave me the last of his Owen treasures, the little statue of Hermes which Owen probably bought in Scarborough in 1918. It seems a poor return that this book quotes some previously unpublished comments in which Owen speaks unkindly about his civilian cousin. Leslie Gunston was a warm-hearted, generous man, and Owen always thought of him as a close and trusted friend. The political and literary gap which opened up between them in 1917–18 is an illustration of the larger division between 'the Nation at Home' and 'the Nation Overseas', one of the crucial developments in modern British history. There were misunderstandings on both sides.

My interest in Owen as a research subject began twenty-five years ago, when I read the newly published *Collected Letters*, and I have been ever more grateful since to John Bell for this editing of that inexhaustible volume; he is among the many people who have helped in the preparation of the present book. I am also grateful to Jon Stallworthy, Owen's official biographer and editor, who has been most kind and generous, as always; and to Peter Owen (Colin Owen's son), June Calder (Leslie Gunston's daughter), and David Gunston (Gordon Gunston's son), all of whom have found unpublished illustrations for me and provided information. My typescript was much improved as a result of suggestions by John Onions, Simon Wormleighton, Tom Coulthard, Douglas Kerr, Helen McPhail, and Philip Guest. Canon H.R. Bate kindly talked to me about Owen a few years ago. Michel Roucoux drove me to various places in the Fourth Army's sector east of Amiens. Martin Taylor (Imperial War Museum) drew my attention to material which I would otherwise certainly have missed. My cousin, Patrick Massey, drew the bridge diagram.

I am grateful to all those involved in establishing and maintaining the Owen Collection at Oxford, including Margaret Weedon and Gwen Hampshire, and to Sue Usher and Regan Harper, who have been unfailingly helpful in allowing me access to the collection. Photographs of items at Oxford are by Paul Freestone.

I am also indebted to the many people who have answered enquiries and helped to find illustrations and information, including Simon Blundell (Reform Club), Ricarda Brock and the late Sydney Brock, Sue Furness (Yorkshire Image), Douglas Gill, Richard Perceval Graves, William Graves, Maurice Griffiths (Napier Polytechnic), Michael Irwin, Paul Reed, Robert B. Robertson, Myrtle Streeten, Anthony Streeten, Major Bertie Whitmore (Flanders Tours), Mike Willis (Imperial War Museum), and Lieutenant W.G. Wallace (Burniston Barracks).

For permission to quote copyright material in the text, I am grateful to the Trustees of the Owen Estate for work by Owen; George Sassoon for Siegfried Sassoon's poems, 'News from the Front' and 'Testament'; and Eileen Scott Moncrieff for the sonnet by Charles Scott Moncrieff and for an extract from his May 1918 letter to Owen.

Acknowledgements for illustrations are shown in the list of illustrations starting on page 214.

LIST OF ILLUSTRATIONS

Sources and copyright holders are shown in brackets. The originals of illustrations marked 'OC' and 'LG' are in the Owen Collection, English Faculty Library, Oxford, among the material donated by Mrs Harold Owen in 1975 and later and by Leslie Gunston in 1978 and later, and are reproduced by permission of the Trustees of the Owen Estate. Some of these items have recently been recatalogued; the new identification numbers are given below. 'BL' indicates manuscripts in the British Library, reproduced by permission of the British Library and the Trustees of the Owen Estate. 'IWM' indicates material in the Imperial War Museum, London, reproduced by permission of the Trustees of the Museum.

Chapter Three: Light Duties

Chapter Four: Training Again

Chapter Five: General Service

Chapter Six: Return to France

Maps and diagram

INDEX